Sacramento Eats

Recipes from the Capital Region's Favorite Restaurants

By Benjy Egel
With a foreword by Mulvaney's B&L
owners Patrick and Bobbin Mulvaney

THE SACRAMENTO BEE

Introduction

California's capital city sits at the confluence of the Sacramento and American rivers, surrounded by farmland, history and political ambition. Occasionally called "the most Midwestern city in California," Sacramento is a mosaic of tourist destinations such as Old Sacramento and residential neighborhoods, where relatively low (but rising) housing prices have made many homeownership dreams a reality. The city houses about 525,000 people, and Sacramento's metropolitan region swells to 2.4 million with the inclusion of its sneakily vibrant suburbs. There's the college town of Davis and its historically Latino neighbor of Woodland to the west, Elk Grove with nearly 200,000 people and its wealth of Asian cuisines to the south and rapidly growing Roseville and Folsom to the east. Most of the U.S.' sushi rice is grown north of the city, while wine grapes, pears and even caviar produced in the nearby Sacramento-San Joaquin Delta make their way to tables around the country.

Sacramento's culinary history begins with the Nisenan tribe, original inhabitants whose food systems included freshwater fish, acorns, berries and wild game. A settler named John Sutter then colonized the city in 1839 after arriving at that confluence of the Sacramento and American rivers. Even though Sutter's Fort was founded in midtown Sacramento (then known as "Rancho Nueva Helvetia") as an agricultural outpost, it became a jumping-off point of the Gold Rush within a decade. Spongy bread, beef and tamales fed the Fort, and the fledgling bar scene flourished to the point that Mark Twain, in a 1866 letter, called Sacramento the "City of Saloons."

Black, Chinese and Mexican residents built up corners of Sacramento's dining scene in the early 20th century, and refined restaurants flourished in areas such as Arden Arcade's "Gourmet Gulch." Yet for most of the 1900s, calling Sacramento's food scene the envy of cities elsewhere would be a stretch. As San Francisco emerged as a culinary beacon two hours southwest, Sacramento was more of an afterthought, a sleepy government town with a reputation for meat-and-potatoes dishes and Capitol business more so than pleasure. As Joan Didion said, "anybody who talks about California hedonism has never spent a Christmas in Sacramento."

I was born in Land Park, a leafy Sacramento neighborhood separated from the urban core by the street of Broadway. My family moved to the western suburb of Davis when I was 3, and I grew up riding my bike to Dos

Coyotes Border Cafe and requesting trips into Sacramento for annual birthday dinners at Tower Cafe. My parents still worked in state offices during the week, which meant my sister and I spent summer days running around Downtown Plaza, a now-defunct mall where the Sacramento Kings' arena sits today.

I left the region for college in 2012 with no plans to move back. But greater forces were conspiring to change the fabric of Sacramento's core, particularly in the food world.

The farm-to-table movement infiltrated every American city's dining scene over the last decade. And while the branding can be more sizzle than steak, more tagline than tagliatelle, Sacramento's wealth of produce and meat within a 100-mile radius certainly made sourcing locally easy for local chefs. Some of those chefs came from the Bay Area, pushed east by a desire for affordability and a slightly slower pace of life, like so many of greater Sacramento's other new residents. Several more, including Brad Cecchi (Canon) and Craig Takehara (Binchoyaki), had their "Lady Bird" moments, fleeing Sacramento for brighter pastures only to find themselves drawn back home.

Nearby farms are a cornerstone of Sacramento's food scene. Another major strength, one that predates the last decade's dining trends, is the region's cultural diversity. Sacramento County is home to sizable Asian, Latino, Eastern European, Black and Middle Eastern communities, all of whom bring unique viewpoints and cuisines to the regional table. In fact, a 2002 study by Harvard University's Civil Rights Project determined Sacramento was the nation's most diverse city.

Fresh ingredients, varied palates and talented chefs — suddenly, Sacramento became a real place to eat and drink. When I interned at The Sacramento Bee in 2015, I was struck by how much the city had changed and all the planned developments to come. The Kings' new downtown arena was under construction, work lunches at Adamo's Kitchen hit the spot and bars such as The Shady Lady Saloon had made going out fun. A Zócalo margarita was my first legal drink that summer, and it wouldn't be my last.

I finished up at Cal Poly, San Luis Obispo and spent a year covering business in Amarillo, Texas, then came back to cover breaking news at The Bee. My shift started each day at 5:30 a.m., required quick writing and regularly revolved around major stories, perfect for a 23-year-old reporter practicing a "work hard/play hard" lifestyle. The Bee's editors must have gotten used to seeing me come into the newsroom A) with last night's leftovers or B) hungover; either way, I took over the food and drink beat in April 2018 and have been there ever since.

Sacramento's dining scene has earned nationwide acclaim during that time, from Michelin stars to James Beard Award semifinalist nods. It's becoming an increasingly culturally vibrant city full of excellent restaurants both high- and low-end. It still falls under the Bay Area's shadow sometimes, but it shouldn't. Sacramento can stand on its own two feet as a dining destination these days, as the 60 recipes in this cookbook will show.

I asked chefs and owners of greater Sacramento's top restaurants and bars to submit recipes of their choosing for "Sacramento Eats: Recipes from the Capital Region's Favorite Restaurants." Some are the most popular items on their menus, such as Skip's Kitchen's classic hamburger or The Butterscotch Den's freezer martini. Others are favorites the chefs make for their families more frequently than their customers, including Nixtaco Mexican Kitchen & Distillery's cortadillo norteño and Kodaiko Ramen & Bar's spicy-sweet Japanese curry.

The end result is this cookbook that captures the Sacramento food scene in full, showcasing the region's culinary diversity and prowess. While all recipes here have been carefully proofread by myself and The Sacramento Bee's editors, with fact-checking from a team of interns, they're very much the brainchildren of the individual chefs. Now it's your turn to make these dishes yourself. Cook and explore!

BENJY EGEL
FOOD AND DRINK WRITER
FOR THE SACRAMENTO BEE

4

PAUL KITAGAKI JR. / THE BEE

PAUL KITAGAKI JR. / THE BEE

Foreword

On Halloween 2012, surrounded by chefs and farmers in Cesar Chavez Plaza, then-Mayor Kevin Johnson declared Sacramento the Farm-to-Fork Capital of America. Situated in the middle of one of the richest agricultural regions in the world, Sacramento is synonymous with produce. Virtually all of the United States' walnuts and almonds, 95% of its tomatoes and more than 80% of its stone fruits like peaches, apricots and nectarines are sourced from the surrounding Central Valley's fields. With such amazing access to farms right in our backyard, it's no surprise that the food and restaurant scene has become such a vital part of the region's culture. But it wasn't always that way, and for a long time nearly all of what the region grew headed out of town. Building Sacramento's strong food community required a healthy ecosystem. To create that, we needed to grow new relationships rooted in trust.

Second-generation Sacramento farmer Ray Yeung grew heirloom tomatoes in 1990 and focused his shipping efforts on San Francisco. One day he was approached by Jim Mills, a sales manager for Produce Express, who wanted to ensure the best quality fruits and vegetables made their way to Sacramento customers. They struck a deal that allowed Sacramento to get the first crack at tomatoes, with the remaining making it down to the Bay Area. This enabled Yeung to sell all his produce and for Sacramento to have more direct access to the food that surrounded it. As more and more trust grew between farmers and local businesses, more farm names came up on menus, telegraphing the relationship between chef, distributor and grower to an ever-increasing number of diners.

Sacramento began to eat better at restaurants. Meanwhile, the bonds between the community and the farms began to manifest at festivals and farmers markets. These newfound connections spread awareness beyond restaurants and markets and into people's everyday lives, exploding into educational programs such as those run by Soil Born Farms and the Food Literacy Center, as well as several urban farms throughout Sacramento County.

The COVID-19 pandemic struck in 2020, testing this trusted network of farmers, chefs and the people. Empty restaurants, no jobs for cooks, unharvested fields and acute food insecurity forced Family Meal Sacramento to form. Sacramento restaurants made and distributed food to students, seniors and community centers, funded by an outpouring of financial aid from the community. This program not only kept the lights on at more than 40 restaurants during the darkest days of the crisis, it inspired the rest of California to establish a similar program called Great Plates Delivered, which brought more than 38 million meals to seniors throughout the state. The ecosystem prevailed.

Benjy Egel has had a seat at the counter since 2018, helming The Sacramento Bee's food and drink beat and watching as our community has fought to build something about which other regions dream. Through his career, he has grown into another trusted voice about everything coming out of the ground and going on plates in Sacramento. The state of food is being looked at with more scrutiny and understanding than ever before, and he is the person who has the knowledge and, most importantly, the trust of the Sacramento food community.

This timely collection of recipes in "Sacramento Eats: Recipes from the Capital Region's Favorite Restaurants" is a reflection of our trust. This cookbook tells the story of our city, as cooks do, through recipes. As you read the book, you gain access to the people and recipes that have earned Sacramento the title of America's Farm-to-Fork Capital. You learn not only about our community but the "how" and "why" of using local ingredients at their peak, while creating great meals and memories in the process. Get ready to whet your appetite, and start cooking!

BOBBIN AND PATRICK MULVANEY
OWNERS OF MULVANEY'S B&L AND
2018 SACRAMENTANS OF THE YEAR

Table of Contents

CHICKEN-FRIED HOT CAULIFLOWER   17

WARM MUSHROOM SALAD   43

SUKIYAKI UDON   60

SPICY-SWEET JAPANESE CURRY   80

Soups & Stews

9

Sauces

Side Dishes

Entrees

10

NOT YOUR MOM'S MAC   90

STEAK AND ALE PIE   120

STRAWBERRY-BASIL ICE POPS OR SORBET   **138**

WHITE LINEN   **155**

Desserts

Cocktails

Appetizers

13

House of Shah Afghan Urban Eats

Borani banjan

Not a fan of eggplant? Try borani banjan anyway, says House of Shah co-owner Selymon "Sal" Shahsamand, who opened his modern Afghan restaurant with his wife Juliana in her hometown in 2017. Creamy and delicious, it takes flavor from the spiced tomato sauce and gets cooled by multiple layers of yogurt. While House of Shah flexes its fast-casual innovation with items such as chapli kebab burgers and chutney-covered fries, all food is based on recipes from Shahsamand's mother and grandmother — and must meet their approval before going out to the world.

TIME: ABOUT 45 MINUTES
SERVES 4-6

Ingredients

2 Chinese eggplants, thinly sliced lengthwise

2 yellow onions, chopped

2 garlic cloves, minced

1 jalapeño, chopped

1 tablespoon salt

1 tablespoon black pepper

2 tablespoons cumin

2 tablespoons coriander seeds

2 tablespoons tomato paste

14 1/2-ounce can crushed tomatoes

1/4 cup olive oil

1 cup Greek yogurt

2 tablespoons dried mint leaves, crushed

Directions

1.   Heat 3 tablespoons of olive oil in a large pan over medium heat. Add the onions and cook until translucent, about 5-8 minutes. Add the jalapeño, tomato paste and one minced garlic clove, and let that combination cook until fragrant, about 1-2 minutes. Reduce heat to low, add the can of crushed tomatoes and let simmer for about 10 minutes, then remove mixture from pan and set aside.

2.   Add remaining olive oil to the pan and return heat to medium. Fry the eggplant slices in the oil, about 2-3 minutes per side. Once done, let the eggplant rest on a plate with paper towels to allow the oil to drip off.

3.   Combine eggplant slices and tomato sauce in the pan, then mix in salt, black pepper, cumin and coriander. Cover the pan and cook on medium-low heat for about 20 minutes, stirring occasionally.

4.   Mix yogurt with remaining minced garlic, then spoon some of the mixture onto the bottom of the serving plate. Plate the eggplant with some tomato sauce, then drizzle more yogurt mixture on top. Sprinkle with dried mint leaves and enjoy with naan or basmati rice.

House of Shah Afghan Urban Eats
538 Main St., Woodland
(530) 665-6516
houseofshah.com

KEVIN NERI / THE BEE

Nash & Proper

Chicken-fried hot cauliflower

Don't be fooled by the term "chicken-fried": this starter is 100 percent vegan. It's simply cooked in the same manner as Nash & Proper's Nashville-style hot chicken, which propelled Sacramento natives Cecil Rhodes II and Jake Bombard to the top of the city's fried chicken pyramid. Nash & Proper caught fire as a super-popular food truck, then won the Downtown Sacramento Partnership's "Calling All Dreamers" competition in 2019 and opened its K Street restaurant shortly thereafter. That larger kitchen helped Rhodes and Bombard expand their menu to include items such as chicken-fried hot cauliflower, which requires overnight marinating but still takes less time to prepare than Nash & Proper's poultry dishes. Adjust spice levels to your preference, wear an apron and eat shortly after frying.

TIME: 1 HOUR, PLUS OVERNIGHT MARINATING
SERVES 8, OR 4 AS AN ENTREE

Ingredients

For batter

2 cups seasoned flour (all-purpose flour plus 1 teaspoon fine kosher salt and 1 teaspoon black pepper)

1/2 cup hot sauce (Frank's RedHot preferred)

2 tablespoons dark brown sugar

1 cup oat milk

1/4 cup fine kosher salt

3 pounds fresh cauliflower florets

For hot dip

4 tablespoons vegetable oil

3 tablespoons cayenne pepper

2 teaspoons fine kosher salt

1 1/2 teaspoons dark brown sugar

1 teaspoon crushed red pepper

1 teaspoon garlic powder

1/2 teaspoon onion powder

1/4 teaspoon ground cumin

For serving

8 slices white bread (the cheaper the better)

Dill pickles, sliced 1/4-inch thick

Directions

To make the batter

1. In a large bowl, combine 1/2 cup seasoned flour, hot sauce, sugar, oat milk and salt, then whisk until lumps are gone. If too thick, add oat milk until desired thickness. Add cauliflower and let sit at room temperature until ready to fry, or for more flavor, let sit in the fridge overnight.

To make the hot dip

2. Heat the vegetable oil in a saucepan, then add cayenne, salt, sugar, crushed pepper, garlic powder, onion powder and cumin. Stir until fragrant, about a minute, careful not to let spices burn.

For frying

3. Heat tabletop deep fryer or pot of vegetable oil to 350 degrees. Strain excess batter off cauliflower. In batches, quickly dredge the cauliflower in 1 1/2 cups of seasoned flour. Shake off excess and lower cauliflower into oil. Be careful not to crowd the cauliflower, about 10–12 florets at a time. Fry for 5–7 minutes until the cauliflower is golden-brown and tender, then transfer to a paper towel-lined plate and let cool slightly before coating in hot dip.

4. To serve, arrange two pieces of white bread on each plate. Toss cauliflower in the bowl of hot dip until well-coated. Place cauliflower on white bread. Serve with as many pickles as possible.

17

Nash & Proper
1023 K St., Sacramento
Plus food trucks and Local Kitchens food halls in Davis and Roseville
(916) 426-6712
nashandproper.com

KEVIN NERI / THE BEE

Dos Coyotes Border Cafe

Crab and asparagus quesadilla

Dos Coyotes would have probably never existed, at least around these parts, had Bobby Coyote's sister not been pursuing her Ph.D. from UC Davis in the 1980s. But on her recommendation, the Los Angeles native and Santa Fe superfan moved north to open his first restaurant in Davis in 1991, then built it into a regional powerhouse alongside chef Mark Casale. Dos Coyotes constantly throws together cross-cultural creations in the spirit of Southwestern cooking, such as paella burritos, blue corn nachos or teriyaki chicken salad over a warm tortilla. Seasonal specials are always worth checking out, including this seafood-and-veggie quesadilla, which has experimented with different fillings over the years yet remains a fan favorite.

TIME: 25 MINUTES
SERVES 12, OR 4 AS AN ENTREE

Ingredients

1 bunch medium asparagus, stems trimmed

2 tablespoons olive oil

1/2 cup roasted red bell peppers, diced

Four 10-inch flour tortillas (Mi Rancho preferred)

2 cups Hatch chile Jack cheese, shredded (Sierra Nevada Cheese Co. preferred)

4-6 ounces Dungeness crab meat

2 tablespoons unsalted butter

Kosher salt to taste

Black pepper to taste

Directions

1. Arrange the asparagus in a microwave-safe dish, cover and microwave on high until tender-crisp, about 2 minutes. Brush asparagus with 1 tablespoon of the oil.

2. Heat grill on medium-high heat, about 375–400 degrees. Grill the asparagus, flipping occasionally, until lightly charred, about 5 minutes. Cut asparagus into 1-inch pieces and sprinkle with salt and pepper.

3. Lay a tortilla on a work surface and top evenly with 1/2 cup shredded cheese. Add 1/4 of the asparagus, 1/4 of the peppers and 1/4 of the crab meat. Fold tortilla in half to enclose fillings. Repeat with remaining tortillas and ingredients.

4. Melt 1/2 tablespoon of the butter in a large nonstick or cast-iron skillet over medium heat. Cook the quesadilla, flipping once, until the cheese is melted and the tortilla is golden-brown on both sides, about 3 minutes per side. Remove to a cutting board and repeat with the remaining quesadillas.

5. Cut into triangles and serve. Casale recommends it be joined by an arugula salad and chipotle crema.

18

Dos Coyotes Border Cafe
10 area locations, from Davis to Lincoln
doscoyotes.com

KEVIN NERI / THE BEE

Restaurant Josephine

Duck liver mousse with preserved Siberian pine cones

Eric Alexander and Courtney McDonald's love for their family can be felt in every part of their upscale yet charming French bistro with Eastern European influences. Josephine refers both to Eric's great-grandmother, who immigrated from Lithuania, and the couple's daughter Josie, whom they're raising on a five-acre Placer County farm 40 minutes northeast of downtown Sacramento. This appetizer is Restaurant Josephine to the core: classic French gastronomy in the liver mousse, with Eastern European adornments via the preserved baby pine cones. Even though Alexander cooks with duck livers, they're extremely hard to find at local grocery stores, so order online or opt for chicken livers. Most Russian markets sell jars of baby pine cones, which become soft caramel-like blobs when cooked in the syrup, though handy foragers can also find their own in the Sierra Nevada foothills.

TIME: 2 1/2 HOURS, PLUS OVERNIGHT SOAKING
SERVES 10–12

Ingredients

1 pound duck or chicken livers, cleaned and trimmed

2 cups whole milk

1 cup Port

1/4 cup brandy

3 shallots, finely chopped

2 garlic cloves, thinly sliced

2 sprigs fresh thyme, leaves only

4 sticks unsalted butter

5 eggs

1 tablespoon kosher salt

1/4 teaspoon pink curing salt (optional)

1/2 teaspoon black pepper, ground

1 cup duck fat or clarified butter

For serving

1 jar preserved baby pine cones, drained, syrup reserved

Toasted Brioche or country bread, for serving

Petite greens or assorted microgreens to garnish

Chef's notes

Preparation begins the night before, when the duck livers soak in whole milk to mellow the flavor and pull out impurities.

Directions

1. The night before proceeding with this recipe, cover duck livers with whole milk and refrigerate overnight. The next day, drain off the milk and discard.

2. Rinse livers and pat dry. Allow livers and eggs to come to room temperature. Lightly oil an enamel terrine mold or small loaf pan with cooking spray, then gently line it with plastic wrap, leaving a bit of overhang. Preheat the oven to 300 degrees.

3. Pour the Port and brandy into a non-reactive pot with the shallots, garlic and thyme. Bring the mixture to a simmer and reduce until syrupy, then allow it to cool. Meanwhile, slowly heat the butter until it is just melted, still emulsified and pourable.

continued >

Duck liver mousse with preserved Siberian pine cones (continued)

4. In a blender, combine the livers, the port/shallot mixture, salt, black pepper and pink salt (if using). Blend on high until puréed. Lower the speed of the blender and slowly pour in the melted butter. Once combined, add in one egg at a time until the mixture is cohesive.

5. Strain mousse mixture through fine sieve into the prepared mold. Cover the mold with a lid or aluminum foil and place in a large roasting pan. Pour very hot water in a roasting pan until it reaches halfway up the side of the mold. Transfer pan to the preheated oven and cook for about 1 hour or until mousse is set. Remove mold from pan and let it cool completely.

6. Melt duck fat or clarified butter until just warm. Once mousse is cool, gently scrape away any discolored skin that may have formed on top and smooth the top layer back out. Pour duck fat or butter in an even 1/4-inch layer over mousse, completely covering it to prevent further discoloration. Refrigerate until ready to serve.

7. To serve, place upside down on a cutting board and remove the mold, keeping the plastic wrap on the mousse as you lift. Gently remove the plastic wrap once the mold has been separated.

8. Using a thin, sharp knife, cut 1-inch slices of the mousse and place in the center of a plate. Slice two pine cones in half per slice of mousse, arrange on and around the mousse and drizzle some of the syrup over the top. Garnish with the petite greens and serve with toast on the side.

Restaurant Josephine
1226 Lincoln Way, Auburn
(530) 820-3523
josephineauburn.com

XAVIER MASCAREÑAS / THE BEE

Milestone Restaurant & Cocktail Bar

Fried green tomatoes

Few restaurants can capture as broad of an audience as Milestone, Nick Dedier and Alexa Hazelton's eight-year-old New American spot in the El Dorado Hills Town Center. It's upscale but not exclusive, familiar yet thoughtful, a place where Saturday night anniversary dinners give way to "weekend hangover brunch fries" on Sunday mornings. The couple, who also owns gluten-free Almighty Food Co. in El Dorado Hills and chicken-focused Chx Shop in Cameron Park, serves this Southern-inspired summer starter over mixed greens with a blue cheese dressing. You can make the green goddess dressing from scratch, or cut out half the work by purchasing a bottle of ranch. Dedier recommends deep-frying the tomatoes in peanut oil, which can be strained and reused after you're done, but pan-frying and flipping will work as well.

TIME: 30 MINUTES
SERVES 8-10 AS AN APPETIZER OR 4-6 AS A MAIN

Ingredients

For green goddess dressing

16 ounces bottled ranch dressing

1 bunch green onions

1/2 bunch parsley

2 garlic cloves

1 tablespoon lemon juice

1 teaspoon onion powder

OR

1 cup mayonnaise

1 cup buttermilk

1 tablespoon fresh dill, minced

6 garlic cloves

1/2 cup white onion, minced

2 tablespoons white wine vinegar

1 teaspoon salt

1 teaspoon black pepper

1 tablespoon lemon juice

1 bunch green onions

1/2 bunch parsley

For remoulade

1 cup green goddess dressing

2 garlic cloves, minced

1/2 shallot, minced

3 Fuji apples

3 celery ribs, diced

1/2 red onion, diced

4 eggs

2 tablespoons distilled white vinegar

Pinch of salt

1/4 cup honey

For frying

8 cups peanut oil

4 green tomatoes, cut into 1/3-inch slices (about 4–5 slices per tomato)

4 cups all-purpose flour

4 cups buttermilk

2 cups Panko bread crumbs

Hot sauce to taste

Old Bay seasoning to taste

For garnish

1/4 bunch of micro cilantro, roughly chopped or 1 shallot, thinly shaved

23

Milestone Restaurant & Cocktail Bar
4359 Town Center Blvd., Suite 116, El Dorado Hills
(916) 934-0790
milestoneedh.com

continued >

24

Fried green tomatoes (continued)

Directions

For the dressing

1. For either green goddess recipe, place all ingredients in a food processor, blender or (ideally) use an immersion blender. Purée until smooth.

For the remoulade

2. Fill a small pot about 80% of the way up with water and a pinch of salt, then add vinegar. Heat the solution to a rolling boil.

3. Add the eggs, still in their shells, and set a timer for 10 minutes. Allow the water to come to a simmer, not a violent boil but still hot. After 10 minutes, remove the eggs from the hot water with a slotted spoon and submerge in ice water. Allow them to cool completely, then peel and dice.

4. Mix all ingredients except the apples together. Dice the apples, discarding the cores, and incorporate them into the mix. Reserve the remoulade for later.

> **Chef's notes**
>
> Be sure to dice the apples and add them to the remoulade only after all other ingredients are mixed. Doing so earlier may cause them to brown.

For frying

5. Create the breading station with 2 cups of flour in one bowl, buttermilk, hot sauce and Old Bay in a second bowl and 2 cups of flour plus Panko bread crumbs in the third bowl.

6. Coat tomato slices in flour one by one. Allow them to rest on a tray while you do the whole batch. By the time you're done with the last slice, the flour on the first one should be sufficiently incorporated with the tomato's moisture.

7. Transfer one tomato slice from the resting tray to the buttermilk solution. Using one hand, turn them to be fully coated in the liquid. Transfer that slice to the panko/flour bowl and coat it thoroughly with your other hand. Don't be afraid to press a little; you don't want the batter falling off. Return the finished slice of tomato to the resting tray. Repeat with all other tomato slices until finished, then allow them to rest for 5–10 minutes before continuing.

8. While tomatoes are resting, heat oil to 350 degrees in a 4-quart pot or Dutch oven, about halfway up the sides.

9. Pick up a tomato slice. If you lose any breading, just plop it back into the dry mix and compensate wherever moisture or gravity has betrayed you. Gently place it into your oil. Repeat with your other slices until you have an even, single layer of tomatoes deep-frying. You should start seeing some color after about a minute. Flip the tomatoes if you think they aren't browning evenly on top or bottom, and remove after about 3 minutes total. A good rule of thumb is to watch the bubbles. Once they stop being aggressive, most of your moisture has evaporated and the cooking process is done.

10. Transfer fried tomatoes to a resting tray and repeat the frying process with all remaining tomatoes. Plate the tomatoes in a line, on a round or on a platter.

11. Put one generous spoonful of remoulade on each tomato slice. If you like it saucy, spoon a little more green goddess dressing over the top. Garnish with micro cilantro or shallots and serve hot. Dedier recommends serving these tomatoes with a mixed green salad topped with blue cheese dressing for a Waldorf-esque feel.

Prahok k'tis

Southeast Asian street food gets restaurant presentation at S.E.A. Hut, Mora and Yom Som's Thai/Cambodian/Vietnamese joint in Elk Grove's Emerald Park Plaza. Opened in 2018, it's split between heartier entrees and snackable items geared toward nearby middle schoolers. Prahok k'tis falls into the latter camp, a vibrant dip with nuanced flavors and no shortage of heat. This dish calls for a lemongrass paste called kroeung, which is ubiquitous in Cambodian food and detailed in its own recipe below. The titular prahok, a fermented fish paste, can be found along with pea eggplants (also known as turkey berries) at Asian grocery stores such as Chhun's Supermarket in south Sacramento.

TIME: 1 HOUR AND 15 MINUTES, INCLUDING 45 MINUTES OF PREP
SERVES 3-4

Ingredients

2 pounds ground chicken or pork

7 ounces coconut milk

2 tablespoons cooking oil (vegetable, corn or soybean)

1 1/3 tablespoons coconut cream powder

4 tablespoons prahok (preferably N&P's Mud Fish Sauce)

2 1/2 teaspoons MSG (optional)

3 teaspoons brown sugar

1/4 cup granulated sugar

2 1/2 teaspoons chicken bouillon

1 ounce tamarind powder

10–15 Thai chiles

10 makrut lime leaves

2 cups pea eggplants

Kroeung

For kroeung

1/3 cup lemongrass, sliced

5 makrut lime leaves, thinly sliced

5 garlic cloves

1/2 ounce fresh galangal, sliced

1 teaspoon turmeric powder

1 1/4 teaspoons curry powder

1 teaspoon paprika

3/4 teaspoon cayenne powder

1 tablespoon red shallots, sliced

Directions

1. Blend all the kroeung ingredients together in a food processor or pound in a mortar. Set aside.

2. Heat a dry skillet on medium heat and add pea eggplants, makrut lime leaves and 10 Thai chiles. Roast, constantly stirring, for about 10 minutes, then remove and reserve for later.

S.E.A. Hut
9655 Elk Grove Florin Road, Suite 3, Elk Grove
(916) 896-1858
seahuteg.com

COURTESY OF S.E.A. HUT

COURTESY OF S.E.A. HUT

3. Add your cooking oil of choice to the skillet and let heat, then add the meat, chicken bouillon, MSG and half the granulated sugar. Fry until the meat is cooked, about 15 minutes, and set aside.

4. In a separate skillet, heat up the prahok with 1 ounce water and add the brown sugar. Stir for about 5 minutes or until the liquid is drained. Remove from heat.

5. Add tamarind powder to the prahok and stir until mixed well. Turn heat back on to medium-low and add kroeung and roasted makrut lime leaves to the prahok mix.

6. Add half of the coconut milk to the prahok mix and bring it to a boil. Add the cooked ground meat to the prahok/coconut milk mixture. Stirring constantly, add the remaining coconut milk and the coconut cream powder.

7. Add the remaining granulated sugar and pea eggplants until the pea eggplants turn olive green, then turn off heat and add the roasted chiles. Chop the 5 remaining Thai chiles, if using, and garnish. Serve over/alongside jasmine rice, sliced cucumber, Thai eggplant, cabbage wedges or long beans.

Franquette

Quiche

In the heart of the Bridge District, a rapidly growing stretch of West Sacramento dotted with condominium buildings and entertainment venues, Franquette quaintly offers a sunny, French-inspired cafe. Married couple Elena and Jack Winks run the kitchen and bar programs at this more laid-back sister concept to Canon in East Sacramento. That means straightforward but technically excellent pastries from Elena, Canon's former pastry chef who attended culinary school in Paris, alongside carefully-curated wines and coffee drinks. This asparagus quiche has become one of Franquette's signature dishes since it opened in February 2022; make it at home for a Sunday brunch, afternoon treat or dinner opener.

TIME: 2 1/2 HOURS
SERVES 6–8

Ingredients

For quiche dough

2 cups all-purpose flour

1/2 teaspoon salt

2 sticks butter, cubed and frozen

1/2 cup ice water

1/4 cup sugar

1 pound dried beans or pie weights

For quiche filling

7 eggs

3 cups heavy cream

3 German Butterball or yellow waxy potatoes

1/4 cup leeks, thinly sliced

1/4 cup asparagus, thinly sliced

8 ounces Gruyere cheese, shredded

2 teaspoons salt

1/8 teaspoon black pepper

Directions

Make the dough

1. Mix butter, flour, sugar and salt in a food processor until the resulting dough looks like sand. Add ice water and pulse until the dough barely comes together, then throw onto a floured surface and knead just enough for it to come together and be smooth.

2. Chill the dough for 1 hour, then roll into a circle with a 12-inch diameter. Return the dough to the refrigerator to keep it cold.

3. Spray a 9-inch round baking dish with 2-inch-tall sides (or a tart mold with 2-inch-tall sides) with cooking spray. Transfer rolled-out dough to a baking dish, gently pressing the dough into the dish so it is molded to fit. Excess dough should flop over the edges of the dish. If any holes occur, patch them with excess dough.

4. Preheat the oven to 400 degrees. Line the dough in the baking dash with parchment paper or aluminum foil. On top of the paper or foil, fill the dish to the top with baking beans or pie weights.

5. Bake at 400 degrees for 15 minutes. Remove from the oven to cool.

6. Once the foil or parchment has cooled enough to handle with bare hands, carefully lift to remove it and the beans. Leave the baked crust in the pie pan.

Filling

7. Bake potatoes at 400 degrees until soft, about 45 minutes. Cool to room temperature and cut into quarters. Reduce oven temperature to 325 degrees.

8. Combine eggs, cream, salt and pepper together in a mixing bowl. Scatter cut potatoes, leeks and asparagus in the baked quiche crust. Pour egg and cream mixture over the vegetables, filling the baked crust 3/4 of the way. Top with cheese.

9. Bake quiche at 325 degrees for 45 minutes to 1 hour, or until the egg custard has fully set. Let cool fully, cut into desired number of slices and serve.

29

PAUL KITAGAKI JR. / THE BEE

Franquette

965 Bridge St., Suite 100, West Sacramento
(916) 572-0046
hellofranquette.com

Shrimp ceviche

Enrikke Valentino grew up swimming and fishing in the American River with his family. They always brought their own seafood to the river, though, along with the other ingredients required to make ceviche on the spot. Valentino's mother, Mireya Godinez-Valencia, founded Mezcal Grill in 2009 in Natomas north of the city center, then expanded southeast to a second location in Tahoe Park a decade later. Ceviche has been a highlight of the expertly executed menu all the while, and Mezcal Grill has earned a reputation as a sleeper gem among in-the-know Mexican food fans. Eat this dish as a snack during warmer months, or as an appetizer for a fish dinner night.

TIME: 45 MINUTES TO AN HOUR, MOSTLY IN PREP
SERVES 3-5

Ingredients

2 pounds shrimp (21–25 per pound), peeled and deveined

1 large English cucumber, diced in 1/4-inch pieces

1 large red onion, diced in 1/4-inch pieces

2 jalapeños, diced in 1/4-inch pieces

1 mango, diced in 1/4-inch pieces

1 red bell pepper, diced in 1/4-inch pieces

4 ounces Clamato

1 serrano chile, diced in 1/4-inch pieces (optional)

2 cups freshly squeezed lime juice, about 20 limes

2 avocados, diced in 1/3-inch pieces

1/2 bunch cilantro, finely diced

Salt to taste

Pepper to taste

Directions

1. Cut shrimp into 1/4-inch pieces and put into a mixing tray (it will spread the juice around better than a bowl). Add the lime juice and red onion, making sure all the shrimp is covered in the lime juice, then add 3–4 pinches of salt.

2. Once the shrimp starts turning pink, about 20–25 minutes, add the jalapeños, Clamato, red bell pepper, mango, cucumber and serrano chile (if using). Mix well, adding pepper and salt to taste. Let all the ingredients mix and rest together for 15 minutes.

3. Serve and garnish with avocado, cilantro and a lime wedge.

Chef's notes

Valentino recommends serving and scooping with tortilla chips, and adding the serrano if you like a bit more kick.

KEVIN NERI / THE BEE

Mezcal Grill
1620 W. El Camino Ave., Suite 172, Sacramento
(916) 646-4826
5701 Broadway, Suite C, Sacramento
(916) 619-8766
mezcalgrill.net

PAUL KITAGAKI JR. / THE BEE

Salads

Origami Asian Grill

Cold noodle salad

Scott Ostrander and Paul DiPierro left fine dining roots behind to open Origami, their tasty and tasteful tribute to Asian cuisines, in East Sacramento in 2019. Most items are put together in a Chipotle-style assembly line, where customers decide what proteins and veggies will define their banh mi, ramen or rice bowl. This cold somen noodle salad is available as a summer refresher and is hearty enough to stand on its own, though you're welcome to add tofu or meat if you'd like. The yuzu-ginger vinaigrette recipe will make 3 cups, far more than is needed for a single salad, but you can store it in the fridge for about 10–15 days.

TIME: 35–40 MINUTES
SERVES 1

Ingredients

5 1/2 ounces somen wheat noodles

1 1/2 cups carrots, julienned

1 1/2 cups green papaya, julienned

1 tablespoon mint leaves, chiffonade cut

1 tablespoon Thai basil leaves, chiffonade cut

3 cups arugula or mizuna (Japanese arugula)

1/2 cup yuzu-ginger vinaigrette

1 teaspoon kosher salt

2 tablespoons peanuts, toasted

Yuzu-ginger vinaigrette

1/3 cup yuzu juice

3 tablespoons lime juice

3 tablespoons lemon juice

1/3 cup fresh ginger, peeled and chopped

6–9 garlic cloves

1/4 cup shallots, chopped

2 1/4 tablespoons granulated sugar

1 3/4 tablespoons brown sugar

1/2 tablespoon rice vinegar

1/2 teaspoon Dijon mustard

1 Thai chile

1/2 teaspoon kosher salt

2 cups canola salad oil

Directions

1. To make the vinaigrette, combine all ingredients except for the canola oil in a blender. Gradually stream in the canola oil and blend until smooth, about 3–4 minutes. Add salt to taste and let cool.

2. To make the salad, cook somen wheat noodles according to package instructions. Place in a bowl and add carrots, papaya, mint, Thai basil, arugula and salt. Toss with yuzu-ginger vinaigrette and top with toasted peanuts.

Origami Asian Grill
4801 Folsom Blvd., Sacramento
(916) 400-3075
origamiasiangrill.com

RANDALL BENTON / THE BEE

Wally's Cafe

Fattoush salad

Walid "Wally" Matar's twin Lebanese restaurants in Rocklin (there's a third in Emeryville, too, which may or may not have inspired the Pixar movie "WALL-E") are the definition of homey hospitality 30 minutes northeast of downtown Sacramento. Matar or a family member is usually there to greet customers warmly and show them to their seats with a complimentary bowl of lentil soup to start and baklava to finish. The fattoush salad is a citrusy, crunchy bridge between those two, capable of accompanying a larger entree or standing on its own as a main dish. Sumac, a tangy spice often used in salads and marinades, is a key ingredient here: Matar imports the restaurant's supply from his home country of Lebanon.

TIME: 15–20 MINUTES
SERVES 4

Ingredients

2 romaine lettuce hearts, chopped 1/2-inch thick

2 tomatoes, chopped into 3/4- to 1-inch cubes

4 Lebanese cucumbers (also known as Persian cucumbers), sliced in half and chopped 1/4-inch thick

1 red onion, julienned

10–12 mint leaves, finely chopped

2 lemons, juiced

6–7 tablespoons extra virgin olive oil

1 teaspoon sumac

1 teaspoon ground oregano

1/2 teaspoon black pepper

1/2 teaspoon sea salt

2 cups fried pita chips (baked pita chips are an option, but may lack the optimal taste and crunchiness)

Directions

1. Mix the lettuce, tomatoes, cucumber, onion and mint leaves together in a big bowl. Drizzle in the lemon juice and olive oil.

2. Sprinkle the sumac, oregano, pepper and salt into the bowl. Toss and mix all ingredients together.

3. Plate the salad on individual plates and garnish with pita chips. Only mix the pita chips in when you're ready to eat, or they'll turn soggy.

Chef's notes

Drizzle in 2–3 tablespoons of pomegranate molasses for a different taste profile, if you'd like. A recipe can be found on page 79, and most Middle Eastern markets carry bottled versions as well.

36

Wally's Cafe

2110 Sunset Blvd., Suite 600, Rocklin
(916) 580-0850
wallys.cafe
4800 Granite Drive, Suite B11, Rocklin
(916) 824-1201
wallyscafe-granitedrive.com

RENÉE C. BYER / THE BEE

38

Juno's Kitchen & Delicatessen

Kale Caesar

Juno isn't a nickname for Mark Helms, Susan Vasques or any of their bipedal family members. This takeout-only deli in East Sacramento is named after the couple's bull terrier/pit bull mix, who would surely rank the kale Caesar beneath the grilled chicken or pastrami sandwiches that come on house-baked sourdough (available for purchase by the loaf). Nevertheless, it's a tasty salad centered around a superfood, and maybe Juno herself would be drawn to the anchovy vinaigrette. You can add grilled chicken if you'd like more protein, or watermelon radish slices for even more color.

TIME: 25–30 MINUTES
SERVES 4

Ingredients

For croutons

5 slices sourdough bread

1 tablespoon herbs de Provence

2 tablespoons olive oil

For dressing

3 lemons

4 garlic cloves

2 tablespoons Dijon mustard

7 anchovy filets in olive oil

1 large egg yolk

2 cups olive oil

2 tablespoons balsamic vinegar

Salt to taste

For salad

2 pounds flowering kale, chopped, with stems removed

1/2 cup grated Parmesan cheese

Directions

1. Preheat the oven to 350 degrees. Pull sourdough slices into bite-sized pieces, place in a bowl and toss with herbs de Provence and just enough olive oil to saturate the bread. Arrange on a baking tray and bake for 7 minutes, or until medium to dark brown.

2. To make the dressing, zest one lemon and juice all three. Add the lemon juice to a food processor along with the zest, garlic, anchovies, egg yolk, mustard and salt. Blend into a paste, slowly drizzle in olive oil to emulsify. Stop the food processor, add the balsamic vinegar and pulse until the dressing reaches the consistency of heavy cream.

3. To make the salad, toss the kale and croutons. Add the dressing to lightly coat the salad, and top with Parmesan.

39

Juno's Kitchen & Delicatessen
3675 J St., Sacramento
(916) 456-4522
junoskitchen.com

AUTUMN PAYNE / THE BEE

Selland's Market-Cafe

Spring pearl couscous

The Sellands go hand-in-hand with Sacramento fine dining and date nights. Selland Family Restaurants owns The Kitchen with its Michelin star, downtown destination Ella Dining Room & Bar and East Sacramento pizza/pasta spot OBO' Italian Table & Bar. The comparatively casual Selland's Market-Cafes, on the other hand, are bright, budget-friendly places where customers of all ages can be easily satisfied. Salads are a particular strength, and this springtime special is a refreshing choice as the Sacramento sun starts shining. It's easiest to approach this recipe in stages, first preparing the couscous to cook before blanching the vegetables and mixing the dressing.

TIME: 25–35 MINUTES
SERVES 4–6

Ingredients

3 cups cooked pearl couscous (recipe follows)

1 cup lemon vinaigrette (recipe follows)

1 cup snap peas, halved on the bias

1 1/2 cups asparagus, cut into 1-inch batons

3 cups zucchini, diced into 3/4-inch pieces

1 1/2 tablespoons fresh dill, chopped

1 1/2 tablespoons mint, chopped

1 1/2 tablespoons parsley, chopped

1 1/2 tablespoons cilantro, chopped

1/2 of a lemon, zested on a microplane

1/2 cup freshly grated Parmesan cheese

Salt to taste

For couscous

1 cup pearl couscous (also known as Israeli couscous)

1 1/4 cup water

1/2 of a lemon, zested on a microplane and juiced

1 teaspoon salt

1/2 tablespoon extra-virgin olive oil

For lemon vinaigrette

1/2 cup fresh lemon juice

1/4 cup canola oil

1/4 cup extra-virgin olive oil

1/2 tablespoon salt

1/4 teaspoon freshly ground black pepper

Salt to taste

Directions

1. To make couscous, in a medium-sized pot, bring water, salt and lemon juice and zest to a simmer. Place couscous in a heat-resistant container and pour the water over the couscous. Cover tightly with plastic wrap and let rest for 10–15 minutes. Strain if necessary, toss with the oil and add additional salt if needed.

2. To make vinaigrette, combine canola and olive oils. Place lemon juice, salt and pepper in a blender. On medium speed, slowly drizzle in oil and emulsify. Add additional salt if needed.

3. In boiling salted water, blanch snap peas, asparagus and zucchini until the color is set, approximately 1 minute, and cool in ice water. Once chilled, strain and dry. Mix in dill, mint, cilantro, parsley, lemon zest and Parmesan and taste for salt.

Selland's Market-Cafe

915 Broadway, Sacramento
(916) 732-3390
5340 H St., Sacramento
(916) 736-3333
4370 Town Center Blvd., Suite 120, El Dorado Hills
(916) 932-5025
sellands.com

LEZLIE STERLING / THE BEE

Kru Contemporary Japanese Cuisine

Warm mushroom salad

Kru emerged as Sacramento's premier sushi spot throughout the 2010s as chef/co-owner Billy Ngo transitioned from wunderkind to seasoned industry veteran. It's not uncommon to see Kings players enjoying hand rolls on their nights off, or couples splurging on omakase service for anniversary celebrations. Yet Kru's cooked items are just as good as the raw options, including this warm mushroom salad. It's been a Kru best-seller since Ngo founded the restaurant in a small midtown space now home to The Jungle Bird, and remains one of customers' top choices in the current, more spacious East Sacramento digs.

TIME: 15–20 MINUTES
SERVES 1

Ingredients

3 ounces mushrooms such as shiitakes, oysters and/or king trumpets

2 ounces Lolla Rossa lettuce, roughly chopped or torn into bite-sized pieces

1 tablespoon unsalted butter

1 teaspoon garlic, grated

1 ounce mirin

Black pepper to taste

Soy sauce to taste

Chives, chopped, to garnish

Directions

1. Clean and cut mushrooms into bite-sized pieces. Heat pan over high heat, add butter and mushrooms and sauté until browned, about 3–5 minutes.

2. Add garlic and mirin and let cook until garlic is cooked through, about 2 minutes. Season with black pepper and soy sauce to taste. Transfer mushrooms over lettuce and garnish with chives.

43

Kru Contemporary Japanese Cuisine
3135 Folsom Blvd., Sacramento
(916) 551-1559
krurestaurant.com

SARA NEVIS / THE BEE

46

Queen Sheba

Awaze beef tibs

A native of Addis Ababa, Ethiopia's capital, Zion Taddese left home at 16 to attend university in London. She fell in love with cooking there while working at her aunt's restaurant, took it over, then left for the U.S. and opened Queen Sheba on Broadway in 2004. It's become Sacramento's flagship East African restaurant in the years since. Meanwhile, Taddese has founded Sheba Farms LLC to promote farming teff, the grain used to make the spongy Ethiopian bread injera, in Northern California. Tibs are pieces of meat cooked somewhere between a stew and a stir-fry, and this classic variation holds a special place in Ethiopian cuisine for its fiery flavors and tender meat, according to Taddese.

TIME: 15–20 MINUTES
SERVES 1–2

Ingredients

1 pound beef, cut into 1-inch cubes

1 large onion, finely chopped

2 tablespoons canola oil

2 tablespoons awaze sauce

2 tablespoons berbere

1 tablespoon ginger, grated

4 garlic cloves, minced

1 teaspoon salt (adjust to taste)

Directions

1. Heat the oil in a large skillet or pot over medium heat. Add the chopped onion and sauté until it becomes soft and translucent.

2. Add the beef to the skillet and cook until it browns evenly, stirring occasionally. This should take around 5–7 minutes.

3. Combine the awaze sauce, berbere, ginger, garlic and salt in a small mixing bowl. Mix well to create a flavorful marinade.

4. Pour the marinade over the beef in the skillet. Stir well to ensure that every piece of beef is coated with the awaze sauce. Reduce the heat to low and let it simmer for about 15–20 minutes, allowing the sauce to infuse into the beef and the meat to become tender.

5. Taste the dish and adjust the seasoning if needed, adding more salt or berbere according to your preference.

6. Once the beef is cooked to your desired tenderness and the flavors have melded, remove the skillet from the heat. Serve hot accompanied by injera, rice or your choice of side dish.

47

Chef's notes

You can use any type of beef here, Taddese said, as long as you can cut it into appropriate cubes. Queen Sheba sells its own injera and awaze sauce to-go (both are also carried in a few local specialty grocery stores), while berbere is sold at many supermarkets.

Queen Sheba
1704 Broadway, Sacramento
(916) 446-1223
queenshebas.com

Beef birria tacos with salsa de arbol

How much does Lisandro "Chando" Madrigal love birria? He once ate it for breakfast every day for a year while living in Tijuana, not missing a single morning. Madrigal honed his skills at backyard cookouts and office parties before quitting his job at Apple to open the first Chando's Tacos truck in 2010. Chando's has opened seven brick-and-mortar taquerias around the region since then, plus two in Georgia. These birria tacos can easily be adapted to meet the quesabirria craze, or eaten sans tortilla like a stew.

TIME: 2 1/2–3 HOURS, PLUS AT LEAST 2 HOURS FOR MARINATING
SERVES 6–8 PEOPLE

48

Ingredients

5 pounds chuck roast or beef shanks, preferably fattier meat

Garlic salt to taste

3 dry pasilla chiles, cleaned and de-seeded

12 dry Anaheim chiles, cleaned and de-seeded

3 Roma tomatoes

1/2 yellow or white onion

4 garlic cloves

3 serrano chiles

1 teaspoon ground cumin

1 teaspoon ground cloves

2 tablespoons dried oregano

2 teaspoons ground pepper

1 tablespoon salt

Water, amount varying

24 tortillas, preferably corn

For garnish

1 bunch cilantro, chopped

1 white onion, diced

For the chile de arbol salsa

8 dry chiles de arbol

2 garlic cloves

1/4 yellow or white onion

1/2 cup olive oil

Salt to taste

Directions

1. Rinse the meat and cut it into 3-inch chunks. If using beef shanks, leave them as they are. Sprinkle garlic salt over the meat according to your preference and set it aside.

2. In a small pot, add water and the dried pasilla and Anaheim chiles. Bring the water to a boil.

3. In a blender, combine the cumin, cloves, oregano, pepper, tomatoes, onion, garlic, serrano chiles and cooked pasilla and Anaheim chiles, along with the water used for boiling. Blend until you have a thick adobo sauce with about the consistency of marinara.

Chef's notes

To make quesabirria tacos, add shredded Monterey Jack cheese or queso Oaxaca to the red tortillas as they heat on the griddle. Once the cheese is melted and the tortilla is crunchy, add the shredded meat and toppings.

Chando's Tacos
7 area locations, from West Sacramento to Roseville
chandostacos.com

PAUL KITAGAKI JR. / THE BEE

COURTESY OF CHANDO'S TACOS

4.   Pour the adobo sauce over the beef and rub it evenly. Cover the meat and let it marinate for at least 2 hours and up to 24. The longer it marinates, the better it will taste.

5.   Once the meat is ready, choose your preferred cooking method: slow cooker, pressure cooker or stovetop pot. Cook the meat low and slow until it becomes extremely tender, at least 2 hours if using a stovetop pot. Check on it occasionally and make sure it's covered at all times to prevent burning.

6.   Near the end of the birria's cooking process, dip each tortilla in the broth's red grease, separated from the rest of the broth using a ladle or spoon. Heat the tortillas on a griddle on medium-high heat, about 30–35 seconds on each side if you want them soft, or longer for crunchy tacos. Don't be alarmed as the griddle begins smoking.

7.   Once the meat is tender, remove it from the cooking vessel and shred it, either by hand or using a fork and knife. Set it back into the pot.

For the chile de arbol salsa

8.   Heat the olive oil in a pan over medium-high heat and add the chiles de arbol, garlic and onion. Cook until they turn brown, about 3 minutes.

9.   Transfer all the ingredients to a blender, add salt and blend until you achieve the desired consistency. Add more olive oil if you prefer a thinner salsa. Taste before serving and adjust the salt if needed.

Assembly

10.   To assemble the tacos, place the shredded birria meat on the prepared red tortillas. Top with cilantro, onion and chile de arbol salsa.

Noroc Restaurant

Borscht

Formerly known as Firebird Russian Restaurant, Noroc rebranded in 2022 to distance itself from the invasion of Ukraine. The owners' roots are in Moldova, anyway, and chef Maria Savchuk handily prepares dishes from across the former Soviet Union for the tens of thousands of Sacramento County residents with Slavic roots. When Russia invaded, Noroc made its borscht free and asked customers to instead donate what they might spend toward victims of the war, netting more than $1,600 in total. The homey red soup is best enjoyed during chilly nights, even if Sacramento's seem balmy compared to those in Eastern Europe.

TIME: 1 TO 1 1/2 HOURS
SERVES 4-6

Ingredients

1 cup celery, diced

1 cup onions, diced

1 cup cabbage, chopped

2 garlic cloves, grated or pressed

1 tablespoon butter

8 cups water or broth (beef or chicken)

14 1/2-ounce can diced tomatoes

2-3 medium- to large-sized beets, peeled (half grated, half diced)

1-2 medium carrots, peeled and grated

1 medium potato, peeled and diced

1/2 cup fresh dill weed

Salt to taste

Pepper to taste

Optional: bay leaf, green beans, peas, beet greens, shredded pork or pork sausage

Directions

1. Add the butter to a large pot and melt over medium heat. Sauté celery, onions and cabbage in butter until softened, about 5-7 minutes.

2. Add the tomatoes, garlic and water or broth to the pot. Cover and bring to a boil, then reduce heat and let simmer for 15-20 minutes.

3. Add the beets, carrots and potato to the pot, along with a leaf (if using). Simmer until tender, about 30-40 minutes depending on size of the pieces.

4. Remove from heat and stir in the dill weed, salt and pepper. Serve into bowls and enjoy.

51

Chef's notes

This borscht can be taken in a number of different directions depending on the cook's add-ins. If you choose to make additions beyond the bay leaf, sauté them in a pan until cooked to your desired level of tenderness, then add to the soup pot during the final stages.

Noroc Restaurant
4715 Manzanita Ave., Carmichael
(916) 485-7747
norocrestaurant.com

PAUL KITAGAKI JR. / THE BEE

Nixtaco Mexican Kitchen & Distillery

Cortadillo norteño

This beef-and-potato stew doesn't appear on the menu at Nixtaco, the Roseville restaurant and distillery that SFGATE claims is home to Northern California's best tacos. It's a dish from chef/owner Patricio Wise's childhood, a filling meal commonly found in most households where he grew up in the Mexican state of Monterrey. Cortadillo norteño freezes well and can be topped with avocado slices if you have a ripe fruit handy. It's typically served with tortillas, and while Wise recommends flour, Nixtaco's fantastic blue corn tortillas are available for sale in 14-packs at the restaurant.

TIME: 1 HOUR
SERVES 4–6

Ingredients

1 1/2 pounds skirt steak, diced

12 ounces bacon, cut into small pieces

1 medium russet potato, diced

1 medium white onion, diced

2 medium tomatoes, quartered

1 medium serrano chile, halved

1 medium dried ancho chile, soaked in hot water

2 tablespoons cumin seeds

1 tablespoon dried Mexican oregano

2 tablespoons Knorr chicken bouillon, or a bouillon cube of choice

2 garlic cloves

1 bunch fresh cilantro

1 lime

Salt to taste

Directions

1. Place the bacon in a 5-quart pot on the stove. Turn the heat to medium-low and fry, stirring often, until most of the fat is rendered and the bacon has browned and looks crispy.

2. Remove the bacon from the pot using a slotted spoon, leaving the fat behind, and set aside for later. Add the diced potatoes and salt and fry on medium-high heat until crispy, stirring often.

3. Remove the potatoes from the pot using the same slotted spoon, again leaving the fat behind, and set them aside for later. Add the white onion and sauté on medium-low heat, stirring constantly until translucent.

4. Add the skirt steak and stir to blend with the onion and fat. Increase the heat to medium-high and cook until meat starts rendering both fat and water. Continue to cook, stirring often, until all the water cooks off and the rendered fat looks like it has glazed the meat.

Chef's notes

Even though the Knorr brand of bouillon was ubiquitous in Wise's youth (and known as Knorr Suiza), he says to substitute any other stock you may prefer if it's already on your shelves. Omit the serrano if you're not so into spicy food, or add another if you love it.

Nixtaco Mexican Kitchen & Distillery
1805 Cirby Way, Suite 12, Roseville
(916) 771-4165
nixta.co

HECTOR AMEZCUA / THE BEE

HECTOR AMEZCUA / THE BEE

5. While the meat cooks, make the sauce. Add the tomatoes, serrano chile, garlic cloves, cumin, oregano, chicken bouillon and the reconstituted ancho chile to a blender. Discard the chile water, which will be very bitter. Add 1 cup of tap water (omit if using chicken stock) and blend into a uniform red sauce.

6. When the meat looks like it's glazed and the onions are starting to stick to the bottom, stir everything once more, being sure to scrape the bottom to ensure nothing gets left behind. Add the bacon and the potatoes, then add the sauce. Rinse the blender cup with a bit of water and add it to the pot as well so that no sauce is left behind.

7. Stir well to make sure everything is incorporated and top with the cilantro. Reduce heat to low and simmer until the stew thickens, at least 20–30 minutes. Longer is better if you have time, but add water as the stew dries out. This avoids it becoming a "horrible tough mess," in Wise's words.

8. When the stew reaches your desired thickness and consistency, remove from heat and add the juice of one lime. Serve in a bowl or in tortillas, topping with sliced avocado if desired.

54

Tower Cafe

East African lentil soup

There's virtually no part of the world where Tower Cafe won't go. Opened by owner James Seyman in Land Park on Earth Day 1990, it's become one of Sacramento's most beloved restaurants by nature of a garden-like patio and having something for everyone to eat. Chef Joe Pounds turns the globe-trotting menu over frequently, introducing limited-time options such as this East African-inspired lentil soup. It's vegetarian, and a great source of protein and fiber.

TIME: 30 MINUTES
SERVES 6–8

Ingredients

1 pound dried lentils

1 Spanish onion, chopped

3 carrots, diced

5 celery ribs

1 gallon water

3 garlic cloves, chopped

3 tablespoons fresh ginger, peeled and chopped

4 ounces Massaman or Thai yellow curry paste

1 tablespoon sunflower oil

1/4 cup honey

28 ounces coconut milk

1 bunch cilantro

1 1/2 tablespoons kosher salt

Directions

1. Combine the lentils, onion, carrots, celery and water in a large pot and bring to a boil.

2. While waiting for the pot to boil, heat sunflower oil in a sauté pan over high heat. Add garlic, ginger and curry paste and sauté for 3–5 minutes, then add to the soup pot.

3. When the pot has been brought to a boil and the lentils are tender, add the coconut milk, honey, salt and cilantro. Continue cooking for another 5 minutes, then taste and add salt if preferred.

Tower Cafe
1518 Broadway, Sacramento
(916) 441-0222
towercafe.com

PAUL KITAGAKI JR. / THE BEE

Q1227

Jambalaya

Q1227's line of customers normally starts forming even before the refined comfort food restaurant opens at 5 p.m. Named for Quentin "Chef Q" Bennett's birthday on Dec. 27 — the restaurant's opening day, too, in 2019 — it has been the hottest eatery in Placer County ever since. This jambalaya gets a lot of its flavor from Chef Q's Cajun seasoning blend, a mixture of brown sugar, chile powder, salt, oregano, onion, paprika, garlic and other spices that's sold in bottles at the restaurant in Roseville, a fast-growing suburb 25 minutes northeast of Capitol Mall. Be sure to use a large Dutch oven or stock pot, as it will make this sizable mixture easier to stir, and add a bit more liquid if it's too dense for your liking.

TIME: 50 MINUTES
SERVES 8

Ingredients

1 pound boneless skinless chicken thighs, cut into bite-sized pieces

11 ounces fully cooked andouille sausage, sliced

1 pound large shrimp (16–20 count), peeled and deveined

3 tablespoons extra-virgin olive oil

2 tablespoons Chef Q's Cajun seasoning

1 yellow onion, diced

2 green bell peppers, seeded and diced

2 celery ribs, diced

4 garlic cloves, minced

1/2 teaspoon red pepper flakes

1 1/2 cups uncooked long grain white rice, rinsed

1 bay leaf

15-ounce can crushed tomatoes

3 cups low-sodium chicken broth

Green onions, chopped, to garnish

Directions

1. In a medium mixing bowl, toss together the diced chicken with 1 tablespoon of Chef Q's Cajun seasoning.

2. Heat 2 tablespoons of the oil in a large Dutch oven or wide-bottomed (and preferably deep) pot over medium-high heat. Add the chicken and sauté until lightly golden and cooked through. Remove the chicken to a plate.

3. Heat the remaining tablespoon of oil in the same pan. Add the sausage and sauté until lightly browned on both sides, about 2–3 minutes. Remove the sausage and set aside on the plate with the chicken.

Chef's notes

Your choice of rice will really alter the cooking time. Basmati and jasmine rice can cook quickly, so Chef Q recommends checking on the texture at around 7–8 minutes. It's best to stop when the rice is al dente, as it will keep cooking when you add the shrimp and let it sit. Chef Q prefers his rice on the side, with a few saffron threads tossed in while it's cooking to add color and flavor.

PAUL KITAGAKI JR. / THE BEE

Q1227
1465 Eureka Road, Suite 100, Roseville
(916) 899-5146
q1227restaurant.com

56

PAUL KITAGAKI JR. / THE BEE

4. Add the onion, bell pepper and celery to the pan and sauté for 4–5 minutes until the vegetables have softened. Feel free to add a splash more oil if needed.

5. Add the minced garlic, the remaining tablespoon of Cajun seasoning and the red pepper flakes to the pan. Stir together for 30 seconds.

6. Add the rice and toast with the vegetables and spices, stirring for a minute. Then add the bay leaf, tomatoes and broth. Give it a stir, bring it to a simmer, then reduce the heat to low and cover. Cook for about 7–8 minutes, stirring occasionally to make sure the rice isn't sticking to the bottom of the pot, until the rice is al dente.

7. Remove the bay leaf. Add the shrimp to the pan along with the sausage and chicken. Gently stir, cover and turn off the heat. The shrimp will cook through in about 4–5 minutes, and all of the liquid should be absorbed by the rice.

8. Taste the jambalaya and season with extra salt and pepper if desired. Garnish with chopped green onions and serve.

Burger Patch

Plant-based chili

Nothing at Burger Patch contains animal products, but owners Phil and Danea Horn aren't content with just serving vegan customers. The Horns want omnivores to visit their plant-based, gluten-free-friendly midtown Sacramento fast food joint, which opened to long lines in 2019. A winter favorite, this chili works great as a side dish, a main or a topping to slather atop veggie dogs or baked potatoes. It's hearty, spicy, just fine reheated the next day and tasty enough that you won't miss meat.

TIME: 50 MINUTES, INCLUDING 15 MINUTES OF PREP.
SERVES ABOUT 10

Ingredients

2 pounds plant-based ground beef alternative

2 red onions, diced

Three 15 1/2-ounce cans kidney beans

6 ounces tomato paste

15 ounces tomatoes, diced

4 cups + 2 teaspoons water

3 tablespoons apple cider vinegar

2 teaspoons agave nectar

2 teaspoons cornstarch

2/3 cup nutritional yeast flakes

2 tablespoons cumin

1 tablespoon chili powder

1 tablespoon smoked paprika

1 tablespoon dried oregano

1 tablespoon black pepper

2 teaspoons kosher salt

2 teaspoons garlic powder

1/2 teaspoon chipotle powder

2 teaspoons neutral oil
(such as sunflower)

Optional garnishes

Dried or fresh herbs to taste

Plant-based shredded cheese to taste

Plant-based sour cream to taste

Directions

1. Rinse kidney beans under cold water and drain.

2. Heat a Dutch oven or 8-quart (or larger) pot on medium-low heat and add neutral oil. Add diced onions to the pot, plus a pinch of salt, and sauté until translucent.

3. Add plant-based ground beef to pot. Season lightly with salt and pepper. Cook ground beef and onions together while breaking the ground beef down into pea-sized crumbles until browned throughout, approximately 4–5 minutes.

4. Add chili powder, chipotle powder (reduce both for less heat), cumin, smoked paprika, dried oregano, garlic powder, kosher salt, black pepper and nutritional yeast to the pot. Cook for an additional 30 seconds to distribute and toast the spices.

5. Add tomato paste and cook for an additional 30 seconds. Add diced tomatoes with juices, agave, apple cider vinegar and 4 cups of water to the pot. Stir to combine all ingredients. Increase the heat and bring the mixture to a gentle boil.

6. In a small container, whisk cornstarch with 2 teaspoons of water to create a slurry. Mix the cornstarch slurry into the pot while stirring continuously to slightly thicken the chili.

7. Add the rinsed kidney beans to the pot. Bring to a boil for 5 minutes while stirring frequently, then reduce to a simmer and let cook on low for an additional 30 minutes, stirring every 7–10 minutes. For a thicker chili, continue to simmer.

8. Dish up in bowls or over your favorites like a baked potato, french fries or plant-based hot dogs. Add your garnish or garnishes of choice.

Burger Patch
2301 K St., Suite 101, Sacramento
(916) 750-4200
burgerpatch.com

JASON PIERCE / THE BEE

Binchoyaki

Sukiyaki udon

Binchoyaki is best known for its meat skewers, grilled over 900-degree binchotan charcoal and served à la carte. Yet the best way to enjoy Craig Takehara and Toki Sawada's Southside Park izakaya is to take a group and wade through the deep menu, trying items rooted in tradition as well as more creative bites. This dish combines sukiyaki, a sweet take on hot pot most seen during the United States' early Japanese food boom of the 1960s, and kake udon, a soup filled with thick noodles. It can easily be made vegan by omitting the butter at the end.

TIME: 25 MINUTES
SERVES 1

Ingredients

6 ounces soy sauce

6 ounces mirin

6 ounces light brown sugar

1 teaspoon ginger, grated

6 cups water

1 pack frozen udon noodles

1/4 white onion, sliced

1/4 carrot, peeled and sliced

8 ounces bean sprouts

2 shiitake mushrooms, sliced

1 medium garlic clove, minced

1 tablespoon sesame oil

1 tablespoon butter (unsalted preferred)

2 green onions, chopped

Salt to taste

Pepper to taste

Directions

1. Combine the soy sauce, mirin, brown sugar and ginger in a small pot and bring to a simmer. Set aside and let cool.

2. Boil water in a medium-sized pot and add the udon noodles. Cook for 30 seconds, strain and set aside.

3. Heat the sesame oil in a medium-sized nonstick pan to medium heat. Sauté the onion, carrot, mushrooms, garlic and pinches of salt and pepper until ingredients are wilted, about 3–5 minutes. Add the bean sprouts and cook until slightly soft, about 3–5 more minutes.

4. Add the udon noodles, along with a little more salt and pepper. Stir the vegetables and udon until combined, then add three ounces of the sauce and mix well.

5. Once the sauce is combined with the noodles and vegetables, add the butter and mix until melted, then remove from heat and serve on a large plate. Garnish with green onions and enjoy.

Binchoyaki
2226 10th St., Sacramento
(916) 469-9448
binchoyaki.com

RENÉE C. BYER / THE BEE

Sweet corn gazpacho with blue corn truffle tostadas

The Capay Valley was home to the Yocha Dehe Wintun Nation, a tribe of Patwin people, long before it became known for growing the United States' almonds and tomatoes. The tribe continues to have a sizable presence in northern Yolo County as owners of both Cache Creek Casino Resort and Séka Hills, an olive oil brand trusted by professional and amateur chefs across the region. Séka Hills features some Native dishes in the restaurant at its 25,000-acre olive farm, which also bears an olive oil tasting room, with another in Clarksburg's converted Old Sugar Mill and one opening near midtown Sacramento. This recipe calls for not Italian truffles but huitlacoche, a fungus also known as cuitlacoche, corn smut or corn truffle that's available at many Mexican grocery stores. A tortilla press is recommended, but you can flatten your masa balls with a heavy skillet, cutting board or clear dish in a pinch.

TIME: 30–45 MINUTES
SERVES 4–6

Ingredients

For gazpacho

3 ears of raw corn, kernels and juices, reserve 1/3 cup for garnish

1 large or 2 medium yellow heirloom tomatoes, chopped

1 yellow pepper, stemmed, seeded and chopped

1 cup cucumber, peeled and chopped

1/4 cup Séka Hills extra-virgin olive oil

2 tablespoons sherry vinegar

1/2 to 1 teaspoon sea salt

Freshly ground black pepper to taste

For garnish

Reserved corn kernels

1/2 cup cherry tomatoes, sliced

Basil and/or microgreens, chopped

For tortillas

1 1/2 cup Maseca Azul Corn Flour

1/4 teaspoon salt

1 cup warm water or more as needed

For corn truffle tomato salad

2 ears corn kernels, grilled and sliced from the cob

3 tablespoons Séka Hills extra-virgin olive oil

1 1/2 tablespoons freshly squeezed lemon juice

3 garlic cloves finely chopped

1/2 teaspoon kosher salt

1/2 teaspoon freshly ground black pepper

1/2 cup huitlacoche

1 cup cherry or grape tomatoes, halved

1/3 cup fresh basil, chopped

Directions

To make the gazpacho

1.   In a blender, combine the corn, tomato, yellow pepper, cucumber, olive oil, sherry vinegar, and salt and pepper. Blend until smooth and season to taste. Serve with the reserved corn kernels, cherry tomatoes and herbs.

62

Séka Hills Olive Mill & Tasting Room
19326 Road 78, Brooks
(530) 796-2810
sekahills.com

MANNY CRISOSTOMO / THE BEE

COURTESY OF SÉKA HILLS OLIVE MILL & TASTING ROOM

To make tortillas

2.   In a large bowl, add all ingredients and mix with a spatula or clean hands until combined.

3.   Knead with hands until the masa comes together, about 5 minutes. Masa should not crack when you press it with your hands. If it cracks, then it's too dry. Add one tablespoon of warm water at a time to reach the right consistency. The masa should not stick to your hands, either. If it does, then you have added too much water. Add a little bit more maseca to correct this.

4.   Roll masa into about 12 golf ball-sized spheres. Cover with cling wrap or a damp towel to prevent masa from drying. Let rest for 5 minutes.

5.   Heat a comal, griddle or iron skillet on medium-high heat. Place one masa ball on the tortilla press between a freezer plastic bag. Press the top down over the dough to flatten it to about 1/8-inch thick. If you like them thinner, rotate the plastic with the tortilla and press gently one more time.

6.   When the comal is hot, place the tortilla on it gently by hand. Cook for 15 seconds. Using a spatula or your hands, flip the tortilla, then cook for 50–55 seconds more. Turn the tortilla one more time and cook for another 50–55 seconds.

7.   Place the tortillas in a clean kitchen towel and stack them up as you cook them. This will finish the cooking process and will keep the tortillas soft.

To make corn truffle salad

8.   In a large bowl, whisk together the olive oil, lemon juice, garlic, salt and pepper. Gently mix in the cooked corn, huitlacoche, tomatoes and basil. Top each tortilla with approximately 1/4 cup of salad and serve alongside gazpacho.

Basil pesto for pasta with cherry tomatoes

The "Godfather" of Sacramento's restaurant scene, Randy Paragary had already been a man about town for 14 years when he founded his eponymous French/Italian bistro in 1983. Paragary's practiced farm-to-fork cooking well before the concept went mainstream, and became one of the brightest lights of Sacramento's dining scene in the 1980s and '90s. Randy Paragary died of cancer in 2021, but his widow Stacy and longtime chef/business partner Kurt Spataro have kept the restaurant humming with seasonal creations such as this pesto. It's best enjoyed during the summer when basil and tomatoes are at their peak, and can accompany any pasta.

TIME: ABOUT 20 MINUTES
SERVES 2

Ingredients

8 ounces pasta, preferably fresh

2 small garlic cloves

2 cups basil leaves, lightly packed

2/3 ounce blanched raw almonds or pine nuts

1 ounce Parmigiano Reggiano, grated

5 ounces extra-virgin olive oil

2 tablespoons cold butter

1 cup cherry tomatoes, halved (Sweet 100 and Sungold are good choices)

Salt to taste

Directions

1. Bring a small pot of water to a boil. Add the basil leaves and blanch for 10 seconds. Remove immediately and plunge into ice water.

2. When leaves are completely chilled, remove and gently squeeze out excess water. Transfer the basil leaves to a blender along with the garlic, nuts, olive oil and a little salt. Blend the ingredients until completely smooth. Transfer the ingredients to a small bowl and stir in the Parmesan cheese.

3. Place the tomatoes in a separate bowl and dress with 1–2 tablespoons olive oil, plus salt. Stir to combine.

4. Bring a medium pot of salted water to a boil. Cook the fresh pasta in the water for about 3 minutes, or follow the box's instructions if using dried pasta. Add the butter in pieces while shaking the pan to create a creamy emulsion.

5. Add 4–5 tablespoons of pesto and stir to create a creamy, emerald green sauce. Add more sauce if desired and taste for salt.

6. Toss the cooked pasta with the sauce and divide between two serving plates. Garnish with the halved cherry tomatoes.

67

Paragary's
1401 28th St., Sacramento
(916) 457-5737
paragarysmidtown.com

LEZLIE STERLING / THE BEE

Adamo's Kitchen

Bolognese

The Adamo family's humble, brick-walled Italian restaurant is an unsung gem of midtown Sacramento's dining scene. The hand-pressed pasta is among the best in town, especially when paired with wine and olive oil from the family's agritourism operation in Tuscany. Even though this tasty meat sauce can be served over any pasta, Chiara Adamo recommends flat, wide pappardelle noodles. Buy them at the store, or sign up for one of Adamo's pasta-making classes to learn how to prepare your own.

TIME: ABOUT 1 HOUR
SERVES 4–6

Ingredients

1 pound ground beef

1 yellow onion, shredded

2 celery ribs, shredded

1 large carrot, shredded

3/4 cup white wine

3/4 cup heavy cream

20 ounces San Marzano tomatoes, blended

Salt to taste

Pepper to taste

Directions

1. Brown the beef in a large pan on medium to high heat, adding salt and pepper. Remove beef when browned, about 10 minutes, and discard fat.

2. Using the same pan, add onion, celery and carrot, along with more salt and pepper. Sweat vegetables until soft and lightly browned, about 5–10 minutes.

3. Add beef back to the pan with white wine and reduce on high heat until wine is almost completely gone, about 5 minutes.

4. Add cream and reduce on medium heat for 4 minutes. Add San Marzano tomatoes and continue to reduce to desired consistency.

68

Adamo's Kitchen
2107 P St., Sacramento
916-440-9611
adamoskitchen.com

Bacon & Butter

Hollandaise sauce

Hour-long lines often wrap around Bacon & Butter on weekend mornings. People flock to Billy Zoellin and Amber Michel's Tahoe Park brunch spot for uber-fluffy pancakes and XL cinnamon rolls. The siblings, who also own The Green Room in East Sacramento, deploy their rich, delicate hollandaise on grilled cheese benedicts and roasted asparagus, but you can spoon it over fish if making dinner. Michel recommends only making as much hollandaise as you'll use for that meal, as reheating the sauce can cause the butter to separate and give you something closer to mayonnaise.

TIME: 10 MINUTES
SERVES 2

Ingredients

1 egg yolk

4 tablespoons unsalted butter

1 tablespoon lemon juice

1 teaspoon Tabasco sauce

1 tablespoon hot water

Pinch of salt

Directions

1. Melt butter over a double boiler on medium-low heat, whisking occasionally. Remove from heat once the butter has melted, approximately 1 minute.

2. While the melted butter cools slightly, whisk egg yolk and lemon juice together in a separate bowl until smooth, approximately 30 seconds. Return the double boiler of melted butter to medium-low heat. Add the egg yolk/lemon juice mixture to the butter while constantly whisking until it reaches the "ribbon stage," where the solution begins to fall in thick (not coagulated), light yellow ribbons from the whisk.

3. Repeat the process of whisking and evaluating the increased thickness of the sauce for approximately 3 minutes. The sauce will thicken as the egg cooks. You may slowly add hot water as needed to achieve desired consistency.

4. As the sauce approaches its desired thickness, add Tabasco and salt to taste. Serve immediately.

71

Chef's notes

Be cautious of excess heat, as you don't want to scramble the yolk. You can remove the pan from heat, continue whisking the mixture and then return to heat to continue thickening if necessary. But don't let it cool too much, either; the emulsification will only hold at around 120 degrees.

Bacon & Butter

5913 Broadway, Sacramento
(916) 346-4445
baconandbuttersac.com

PAUL KITAGAKI JR. / THE BEE

Cacio

Lamb ragu

Katie Kinner-Kerksieck and Jonathan Kerksieck's relationship is the kind of story Hallmark movies are built on. The couple met while working at downtown restaurant Grange in 2008, Jonathan as the chef de cuisine and Katie as the front-of-house manager, and they bonded over the cacio e pepe he made her early in their courtship. That became the namesake for their snug Italian restaurant in the mostly residential neighborhood of Greenhaven, where the menu changes seasonally. Cacio's owners recommend serving this lamb ragu in spring over a ribbon pasta (pappardelle, fettuccine) or short pasta (penne, fusilli).

TIME: ABOUT 1 HOUR
SERVES 5–6

Ingredients

2 1/2 pounds ground lamb

1 pound onion

1 pound carrots

1 pound celery (about 8 ribs)

1/2 pound fennel

6 garlic cloves

1/4 cup olive oil

1 tablespoon fennel seeds, toasted and ground

1/2 tablespoon fennel pollen

1 cup red wine

28-ounce can of DiNapoli organic whole peeled plum tomatoes

Salt to taste

Pepper to taste

Parmesan cheese, pecorino or ricotta salata to garnish

Directions

1. Heat the olive oil in a 5- or 6-quart pot (stainless steel or enameled preferred) over medium heat. Add lamb to pot and cook, stirring frequently, until the meat is in small brown crumbles, about 10–15 minutes.

2. While the lamb is browning, use a food processor to finely mince the onion, carrots, celery, fennel and garlic.

3. When the lamb has browned, deglaze with red wine and add the vegetables. Stir vegetables and cook into the meat for about 5 minutes.

4. Hand-crush the tomatoes and add to the pot. Stir in fennel seeds and fennel pollen.

5. Turn the heat down to a simmer and continue cooking for about 45 minutes, stirring occasionally so as to not burn the bottom of the pot.

6. Season to taste with salt and pepper, and garnish with your choice of hard cheese.

Chef's notes

Baby spinach, fava beans and artichoke hearts all make nice additions to this sauce. If using, add those in a sauté pan as you toss the pasta and sauce together.

RENÉE C. BYER / THE BEE

Cacio
7600 Greenhaven Drive, Suite 23, Sacramento
(916) 399-9309
caciosacramento.com

72

ANDREW SENG / THE BEE

Mesa Mercado
6241 Fair Oaks Blvd., Carmichael
(916) 283-4081
mesamercado.com

ANDREW SENG / THE BEE

Mesa Mercado

Mole Oaxaqueño

Carmichael's glitzy Milagro Centre revolves around Mesa Mercado, Ernesto Delgado's seven-year-old tribute to the Mexican state of Oaxaca's markets and ingredients. The restaurateur behind Mayahuel, La Cosecha, Sal's Tacos and (soon) Mercado Urbano, Delgado has his own take on one of Oaxaca's most famous dishes — it's not known as "the Land of the Seven Moles" for nothing, after all. Also called mole negro, this intricate sauce uses more than 20 ingredients varying from chiles to animal crackers in order to achieve its nuanced taste. Serve it over enchiladas, poultry, roasted vegetables or anything else that could stand to improve from a velvety, slightly smoky blanket, and freeze what you don't use for future dishes.

TIME: 5–6 HOURS
MAKES 3 QUARTS

Ingredients

3/4 pound pasilla chiles,
stems and seeds removed

3/4 pound ancho chiles,
stems and seeds removed

1/2 pound mulato chiles,
stems and seeds removed

1 1/2 cups pumpkin seeds

1 1/2 cups walnuts

1 cup plus 2 tablespoons peanuts, shelled

3/4 cup almonds

1 1/2 cups plantains, cut into rough, thin slices

1 1/2 apples, cored and cut into rough, thin slices

1 cup prunes

1 cup raisins

6 Nestle Abuelita chocolate tablets
(3.1 ounces apiece)

1 1/2 cups sesame seeds, 3 tablespoons
reserved for garnish

1 2/3 tablespoons black pepper

2 1/4 tablespoons ground cloves

2 1/3 tablespoons cumin

1/3 cup dried oregano

2 cinnamon sticks

2 corn tortillas

1/2 loaf bolillo bread

1/4 pound animal crackers

1 large white onion, sliced

10 garlic cloves

1/2 cup plus 2 teaspoons canola oil

1/2 cup chicken or vegetable broth (optional)

Salt to taste

Directions

1. Heat a dry skillet or comal over medium heat. Toast the pasilla, ancho and mulato chiles until they become fragrant, only about 2–3 seconds, being careful not to burn them. Once toasted, transfer the chiles to a bowl and cover them with hot water. Let them soak for about 30 minutes or until softened.

2. In the same skillet or comal, toast the pumpkin seeds, peanuts, almonds and walnuts until lightly browned and fragrant, about 3 minutes. Remove them from the heat and set aside. In the same skillet or comal, char the onions and garlic for about 10–12 minutes, then set aside. Add a teaspoon of canola oil, then fry the apples and plantains for 10–12 minutes and set aside. Toast the raisins and prunes for about 6 minutes, then set aside. Add another teaspoon of oil, then char the bread and tortillas for about 3 minutes and set aside.

3. Quickly toast the cloves, cumin, black pepper, cinnamon stick and oregano until fragrant, about 3 minutes, then set aside. Using a spice grinder or mortar and pestle, grind the toasted spices into a fine powder.

4. Drain the soaked chile peppers and transfer them to a blender or food processor. Add the toasted seeds and nuts, spice blend, sesame seeds, cinnamon sticks, corn tortillas, bolillo bread, plantains, animal crackers, onions, garlic and apples to the blender. Blend the ingredients until you have a smooth, thick paste. You may need to do this in batches, depending on the size of your blender or food processor.

5. Heat remaining 1/2 cup of oil in a large pot or Dutch oven over medium heat. Carefully pour the blended mole paste into the pot and stir to combine with the oil. Reduce the heat to low and let the mole simmer for 1 1/2 hours, stirring occasionally to prevent sticking. Add the chocolate and let simmer for at least another hour, continuing to stir as needed. The longer you cook the mole, the deeper the flavors will develop. If the mole becomes too thick, you can add some chicken or vegetable broth to adjust the consistency. Season the mole with salt to taste.

6. Once the mole is cooked to your desired consistency and flavor, it is ready to be served. Mole negro is traditionally served over roasted or grilled poultry, such as chicken or turkey. Garnish with toasted sesame seeds.

Masullo Pizza

Persillade dressing

Bobby Masullo grew up in Land Park, left for stints in other cities, then returned to open the neighborhood's top pizzeria (and arguably the best citywide). Masullo's Neapolitan-style pizzas are hard to emulate at home, unless your wood-burning oven gets up to 900 degrees and your dough is made from "mother" that's been fastidiously kept alive for years. The persillade dressing, on the other hand, is simple to construct and will add lots of flavor to salads. It's intended for lettuce, but Masullo has been known to drizzle it atop pizzas as well.

TIME: 15 MINUTES
SERVES 2 FAMILY SIZED DINNER SALADS

Ingredients

For the persillade

5 anchovies

5 garlic cloves

1 bunch of parsley, large stems removed

1/2 cup extra-virgin olive oil

For the dressing

1/2 cup apple cider vinegar

1 cup extra-virgin olive oil

1 teaspoon capers, chopped

1/2 cup persillade

Directions

Make the persillade

1. Chop the anchovies, garlic and parsley in a food processor with half of the olive oil. Once the mixture is well chopped, add in the remaining oil.

2. Place in a fresh container and refrigerate. It will hold for a week.

Make the dressing

3. Mix the vinegar, oil, capers and persillade. Pour atop romaine or other lettuce.

Chef's notes

This dressing's acidity will cause the parsley to fade from bright green to khaki after about a day in the refrigerator. It's a little unsightly, but harmless.

Masullo Pizza
2711 Riverside Blvd., Sacramento
(916) 443-8929
masullopizza.com

DANIEL KIM / THE BEE

SAUCES

77

Tree House Cafe

Pomegranate molasses

Farm-to-fork? At Tree House Cafe, it's more like backyard-to-bite. Longstanding fruit trees shade the tables and supply chef E.B. Shin with fresh produce year-round, along with a perpetually booming garden. Generations of Ulatan family members lived at 630 3rd St. until they rented it to restaurateur Jeff "Fro" Davis on the condition that his restaurant would incorporate fruit from the decades-old trees planted by the family patriarch. That canopy includes two prosperous pomegranate trees as well as the oranges used in this recipe, which can be kept in your refrigerator for months or frozen for longer.

TIME: 2–2 1/2 HOURS
YIELDS 3–4 CUPS

Ingredients

8 cups of pomegranate juice
(roughly 15–18 pomegranates)

1 1/2 cups lemon juice

1 cup orange juice

3 cups cane sugar

1 cinnamon stick

1 teaspoon freshly grated nutmeg

2 teaspoons kosher salt

Chef's notes

You can marinate chicken or fish in pomegranate molasses before grilling, or use it as the base for a salsa atop pork chops. Tree House Cafe slathers it on sourdough for the "My Cousin Vinny" sandwich, which also features apples or Asian pears grown on the property, arugula, melted brie cheese and prosciutto. Shin also likes it as the dressing for a salad featuring arugula, blood oranges and macadamia nuts.

Directions

1. If juicing your own pomegranates, gather all 15–18 and cut each in half. Take a heavy metal or wooden spoon and beat the pomegranates on their exterior side to free the seeds from the pith. This is the fastest way to remove the seeds but can get messy, so strike them into a large bowl. Once all the seeds have been released into the bowl, remove any pith that has been beaten into your bowl, as it'll be bitter and unpleasant.

2. Purée the pomegranate seeds in a food processor until all the liquid leeches out of them. Filter the juice through a fine sieve or Chinois, separating the seeds. Using the back of a spoon or a small ladle, push any juice still clinging to the seeds through the sieve or chinois.

3. Combine pomegranate juice, lemon juice, orange juice, sugar, cinnamon stick and kosher salt in a heavy-bottomed, 4-quart (or larger) pot. Bring the mixture to a boil, then turn the heat down to a gentle simmer. Make sure you're cooking the molasses softly and gently, not boiling it aggressively. The liquid should look like it is slightly dancing in your pot.

4. Let the molasses simmer for 1 1/2 to 2 hours. The molasses is done when it coats the back of a spoon with ease and looks nice and thick.

5. Transfer the molasses into a large bowl and remove the cinnamon stick. Grate fresh nutmeg into the molasses and let it cool.

79

Tree House Cafe
630 3rd St., West Sacramento
(916) 942-9229
thcwestsac.com

LEZLIE STERLING / THE BEE

Kodaiko Ramen & Bar

Spicy-sweet Japanese curry

Kodaiko earned its reputation as arguably Sacramento's best ramen house for its skill at creatively incorporating new flavors. The classic tonkotsu is excellent, but the citrus shio or mushroom paitan with cashew cream shine just as bright. Japanese curries are a story of adaptation as well in the spirit of yōshoku, Western-influenced cuisine that became increasingly popular after World War II. Instant curries from boxes have become Japanese comfort food; Kodaiko chef/partner Takumi Abe's version uses fresh items typically found in most Japanese pantries. Abe's recipe is vegan, though cooks can substitute 8 tablespoons of butter for the two oils if they'd prefer. Serve it over rice with whatever seasonal vegetables strike your fancy.

TIME: ABOUT 2 HOURS
SERVES UP TO 6

80

Ingredients

4 tablespoons sesame oil

4 tablespoons neutral oil (such as canola, vegetable or grapeseed)

1 medium yellow onion, diced

3 medium carrots, all peeled, 1 diced the same size as the onion and other 2 roll-cut

1 pound Yukon gold potato, peeled and cut into bite-sized pieces (about 1-inch)

3 tablespoons ginger plus more to garnish, minced

2 tablespoons garlic, minced

5 tablespoons S&B curry powder

5 ounces mirin

1/3 cup ketchup

1/3 cup Bulldog katsu sauce

1 tablespoon honey

4 cups mushroom or vegetable broth

2 cups filtered water

2 teaspoons cornstarch, mixed with 2 ounces water to create a slurry

3 teaspoons salt, plus more to taste

Pickled onions to garnish

Directions

1. Mix the sesame and neutral oil of your choosing together. Add 4 tablespoons of the resulting mixture to a 6-quart pot over medium heat.

2. When the oil is hot, add the onion and diced carrot with a pinch of salt. Cook until the onions begin to brown and are translucent, about 5–7 minutes, stirring often with a rubber spatula or flat-tipped wooden spoon. You're looking for color on the onions, but not for them to be burnt.

3. Add the rest of the oil. Add the ginger and cook for 1 minute, stirring often so as to not burn it. Add the garlic and cook for another minute, stirring constantly so that it doesn't burn or color. Add the curry powder and stir constantly for a minute to bloom the spices.

Chef's notes

"Seasonal vegetables" means fresh peas (snap, snow or English all work), scallions and asparagus in the spring; summer squash, corn and peppers in the summer; cauliflower, okra and sweet peppers in the fall; and broccoli, kabocha and butternut squash in the winter.

Kodaiko Ramen & Bar
718 K St., Sacramento
(916) 426-8863
kodaikoramen.com

COURTESY OF MATT CHONG

4. Add the mirin, ketchup, katsu sauce and honey. Bring to a boil, turn down to low and stir, scraping the brown bits off the bottom of the pot. Cook for 3 minutes.

5. Add the broth, water, roll-cut carrots and salt. Stir to incorporate, bring to a low boil and cover the pot.

6. Turn the heat down to as low as it can go. Cook for 1 hour, stirring every 10 minutes or so to make sure it is still gently bubbling. You're looking for small bubbles, not a rolling boil.

7. Uncover the pot. Add the potatoes and cornstarch slurry. Turn the heat up to medium-low and bring the curry back to a boil.

8. Cook for 20–30 more minutes uncovered, or until the potatoes are tender and the curry has cooked down to about half of its original volume. As a reference, use the ring on the inside of the pot indicating the curry's original volume.

9. Add the seasonal vegetables if you are using them. Turn off the heat and cover the pot. Let sit for about 5 minutes, depending on the type of vegetables you choose and how small you cut them.

10. Serve in a bowl with a generous ladle of curry atop or aside rice. Garnish with pickled onions and/or ginger.

Side Dishes

Tori's Place

Black-eyed peas

Victoria Haggins' soul food stand in Del Paso Heights doesn't do frills, trends or bland. All it does is Southern hospitality and some of Sacramento's best down-home cooking, offered out of Styrofoam containers with folding chairs for seating. Patrons have salivated for Tori's Place's gumbo and hot water cornbread since Haggins opened up shop across from Grant Union High School in 2012. These black-eyed peas are a thoroughly seasoned side worthy of their own space at the table. Preparing them for New Year's Day is a Southern tradition, but they're just as tasty any time.

TIME: 50 MINUTES TO 1 HOUR
SERVES 6–8

Ingredients

Eight 16-ounce cans black-eyed peas

1 celery rib, chopped into bite-sized pieces

14 1/2-ounce can diced tomatoes

6–12 ounces frozen sliced okra

1 red bell pepper, chopped, seeds and veins removed

1 green bell pepper, chopped, seeds and veins removed

1/2 red onion

1/2 white onion

1 green onion, chopped

6–7 baby carrots, chopped

1 jalapeño, sliced

1/4 cup vegetable oil

Lawry's Seasoned Salt to taste

Black pepper to taste

Onion powder to taste

Parsley leaves to garnish

Directions

1. Combine black-eyed peas, celery, tomatoes, bell peppers, onions, carrots, jalapeño, vegetable oil, Lawry's Seasoned Salt, black pepper and onion powder in a large pot, along with one black-eyed peas can's worth of water.

2. Bring the pot to a simmer and let it cook for 20–30 minutes. Add the okra and let simmer for another 10 minutes. Serve over rice or cornbread, or in a bowl on its own. Garnish with parsley leaves.

85

Tori's Place
1525 Grand Ave., Sacramento
(916) 646-6038
victoriahaggins59.wixsite.com/torishomecooking

Zócalo

Cilantro-lime rice

Rice is an underrated part of a Mexican meal, and Zócalo's stands apart from its competitors. Triangular rice towers dyed green by cilantro-lime pesto accompany most of chef Brian Castillo's creations, from happy hour nibbles to cochinita pibil dinners. It's a side dish yet an understated favorite at Zócalo, which has opened restaurants in four lively districts or shopping centers (the Handle District, The UV, Fountains at Roseville and Broadstone Plaza) since first debuting in 2004.

TIME: 35 MINUTES
SERVES 4

Ingredients

For cilantro-lime pesto

1 ounce fresh lime juice

3–4 garlic cloves

1/3 of a jalapeño

3/4 teaspoon salt

1 bunch cilantro

1/3 cup canola oil

For the rice

4 cups white rice

6 cups water

3/4 teaspoon salt

Directions

Make the cilantro-lime pesto

1. Remove the jalapeño's stem. Discard the seeds and veins if seeking a less-spicy version. Using an immersion blender, blend the lime juice, garlic, jalapeño and salt on high until smooth.

2. Lower the blender to medium, then add in 1/3 of the cilantro at a time, slowly pouring the canola oil in between each bunch. The pesto should be slightly coarse. Set aside and reserve; excess pesto can be used as a dipping sauce or topping.

Make the rice

3. Heat oven to 350 degrees. Rinse the rice and strain. Place the rice into an oven-safe pot and pour in the water and salt. Cover with aluminum foil and bake for 20 minutes. You can also prepare the rice using a rice cooker; follow brand directions to do so.

4. Remove the rice from the oven and add to a mixing bowl, using a large spoon or wooden spatula to break up any lumps. Pour in the pesto, then fold and mix into the rice. The rice should be completely coated with the pesto, turning it from white to green throughout.

86

Zócalo
1801 Capitol Ave., Sacramento
(916) 441-0303
466 Howe Ave., Sacramento
(916) 252-0303
1182 Roseville Parkway, Roseville
(916) 788-0303
2739 E. Bidwell St., Folsom
(916) 618-0303
experiencezocalo.com

AUTUMN PAYNE / THE BEE

Mulvaney's B&L

Grilled asparagus with prosciutto

Patrick Mulvaney might hail from New York, but after 32 years shaping Sacramento's dining scene, he's as 916 as they come. Mulvaney and his wife Bobbin turned an 1890s brick firehouse into Mulvaney's B&L, a Sacramento dining institution with deep local farmer connections and a menu that changes daily. In-the-know customers call ahead to reserve seats for "Family Meals," communal prix fixe dinners with a seasonal theme on the fourth Monday of each month, and the lovely patio attracts business lunches as well as date nights. Patrick Mulvaney is more likely to be found advocating for mental health support within the restaurant industry than butchering a pig these days, but Bobbin's daughter Sarah Wasson has stepped in as Mulvaney's B&L's new managing partner. Look for more dishes highlighting local ingredients such as the Sacramento-San Joaquin Delta's famous (though hard to find — try local farmers markets in the spring) asparagus in years to come.

TIME: 20 MINUTES
SERVES 4

Ingredients

2 bunches Delta asparagus, woody bottoms snapped off

1 lemon, juiced

1/4 cup California olive oil

2–4 eggs, depending on method

4 thin slices of prosciutto

Chef's notes

Hard-boiled eggs are simpler, but Mulvaney's "jewel box" eggs only take a bit more work and will give you runny, eye-catching dipping baskets. You can prepare the asparagus ahead of time, refrigerate and serve it cold if headed to a summer party — "grilled and chilled," as the chef says. Mulvaney's B&L has frequently tweaked the specifics of this dish over the years, with other renditions featuring sunny side up eggs (as pictured) or a Nantes carrot emulsion.

Directions

1. Heat the grill and oil it, along with the asparagus. Grill the asparagus, rotating, until the spears are lightly charred, about 2 to 3 minutes depending on grill temperature. Remove the asparagus when al dente, as it'll continue to cook.

2. Place the spears facing one direction on a small oval plate and dress with lemon and oil. Prosciutto can be laid flat underneath or in a bundle on the side of the asparagus. Top with hard-boiled eggs, if using, or serve alongside jewel-box eggs.

If hard-boiling eggs

3. Put 2 eggs in a pot with cold water. Bring to a boil, remove from heat, cover and let sit for 10 minutes. Remove from water, peel and coarsely chop. You can separate the whites and yolks to keep the colors distinct.

If preparing them jewel-box style

4. Boil 4 eggs for 5 1/2 minutes, then submerge in ice water. Peel and refrigerate.

5. When ready for service, warm eggs slightly in boiling water or oven. Cut the tops off to make egg baskets so you can dip the asparagus in the runny yolks.

89

Mulvaney's B&L
1215 19th St., Sacramento
(916) 441-6022
mulvaneysbl.com

CARL COSTAS / THE BEE

The Rind

Not your mom's mac

Sara Arbabian's midtown restaurant is Sacramento's home for all things dairy, from exquisite grilled cheese sandwiches to artistically arranged boards of gouda and chèvre. If there's a star dish at The Rind, it's the fancified macaroni and cheese, rich and encrusted with a layer of gratin. Make it as a cookout side, or add some ham or prosciutto and call it a hearty weeknight dinner. Get your pasta water boiling first, then start making the béchamel, a French "mother sauce" that provides macaroni and cheese's creamy texture.

TIME: ABOUT 1 HOUR 15 MINUTES
SERVES 6–8

Ingredients

12 ounces sharp white cheddar, shredded

12 ounces young Gruyere (aged 4 months), shredded

12 ounces Parmigiano Reggiano, shredded

20 ounces dry pasta of choice

2 slices sourdough bread

1 3/4 tablespoons fresh parsley

1 2/3 tablespoons fresh thyme

2 1/3 tablespoons fresh oregano

4 cups whole milk

1/4 yellow onion, diced

1/4 shallot, diced

1 bay leaf

2 whole cloves

1 stick butter

1 1/2 tablespoons all-purpose flour

1/2 tablespoon kosher salt

1/3 teaspoon ground nutmeg

1/3 teaspoon ground white pepper

1/2 tablespoon Tapatío hot sauce

Directions

1. Bring a large pot of salted water to a boil. Cook the pasta according to package directions, removing and straining it when al dente.

2. In a stockpot, melt butter on medium-high heat. Add the onion, shallot, cloves and bay leaf. Heat until slightly softened and translucent, about 5 minutes.

3. Add flour using a large whisk. Cook flour down until bubbly to create a roux, about 5 minutes.

4. Slowly add 1/4 of the cold milk to the hot roux, whisking it in. Continue whisking until thickened. Repeat by adding another 1/4 of the milk. Continue to add milk in small batches until milk comes to temperature and béchamel is thickened, whisking all the while.

Chef's notes

There's no fancy pasta barrier that would prevent home cooks from preparing this recipe. The Rind uses Barilla's Campanelle noodles, bellflower-shaped beauties that can be found at most grocery stores.

The Rind
1801 L St., Suite 40, Sacramento
(916) 441-7463
therindsacramento.com

90

RANDALL BENTON / THE BEE

5. Lower heat to medium-low and cook for an additional 15–20 minutes. Season with Tapatio, nutmeg, salt and white pepper to taste.

6. Strain mixture through a Chinois into a heat-safe container. Pour back into the pot. Add shredded cheese in small batches on medium heat, stirring constantly. Continue to add shredded cheese until all is incorporated.

7. Preheat the oven to 350 degrees. Pour cooked noodles into a 9x13-inch baking dish of choice. Slowly pour cheese sauce over and mix well.

8. Bake pasta for 15 minutes or until just before bubbling. While pasta is baking, toast sourdough slices in the oven for 5–10 minutes. Remove and blend in a food processor with parsley, thyme and oregano. Remove the pasta and finish it with the bread crumb mixture, then serve.

Localis

Antonio's tawny duck

Localis chef/owner/beverage director Chris Barnum-Dann put a glass of tawny port to his lips on a visit to Quinta do Javali, a Portuguese winery. Within minutes, he had concocted this duck confit dish, named for third-generation winery owner Antonio Mendes, to go with that wine. Barnum-Dann's Michelin-starred restaurant featured Antonio's tawny duck on its June 2023 menu dedicated to the foods and drinks of Portugal. Other menus have highlighted the Placer County-born chef's travels to Peru, Spain and Thailand, but Barnum-Dann makes sure to highlight Localis' use of local growers such as Riverdog Farm in Guinda or Twin Peaks Orchards in Newcastle.

TIME: 2 DAYS OF PREP AND IDLE TIME, 25 MINUTES AT TIME OF SERVICE
SERVES AT LEAST 4

Ingredients

2 duck legs

2 duck breasts

For the brine (legs)

3 1/4 cups water

3 1/3 tablespoons kosher salt

2 sprigs whole fresh lavender

1 3/4 teaspoons black peppercorns

2 bay leaves

1 pint duck fat

1 guajillo chile

1 tablespoon fennel seeds

1 tablespoon wild honey

2 tablespoons neutral oil
(such as corn or vegetable)

For the cure (breasts)

4 tablespoons kosher salt

3 tablespoons sugar

1 large lavender sprig

1 tablespoon chervil

1 1/2 teaspoons sage

1 teaspoon oregano

3/4 teaspoon green peppercorns

Directions

For the brine (legs)

1. Lightly toast fennel seeds and peppercorns in a medium pot until just fragrant. Pour in water, followed by all other brine ingredients. Bring to a simmer and chill as quickly as possible in an ice bath.

2. Cover duck legs with chilled brine and refrigerate for 30 hours. Drain and rinse the legs, and set them on a pan rack with linens underneath. Leave in the refrigerator for 24 hours to let a pellicle (thin skin) form.

3. Heat the oven to 250 degrees. Melt enough duck fat in a pot over low heat to cover the legs, then cook in the oven for about 6 hours until the duck is tender and falls off a testing poker freely.

4. Let the duck cool in the fat. When warm, debone the leg meat and press it between two flat surfaces to sear off in a pan later. Preserve the meat in its fat in the refrigerator for up to 2 months.

Chef's notes

Duck fat should be available at most grocery stores, from Safeway to your local natural foods co-op. A pan rack refers to a baking rack with a cooking sheet underneath. Serve with roasted seasonal vegetables and a grain of some sort — Barnum-Dann likes farro or spelt, in this case.

Localis
2031 S St., Sacramento
(916) 737-7699
localissacramento.com

HECTOR AMEZCUA / THE BEE

COURTESY OF LOCALIS

5. When ready to serve, preheat an oven to 450 degrees. Heat a cast iron skillet very high and coat the bottom with neutral oil. Sear the duck in the skillet for two minutes on each side, then finish it for approximately 10 minutes in the oven.

For the cure (breasts)

6. Bring all ingredients, aside from the duck, together in a food processor and pulse until fully incorporated. Cover breasts in the resulting cure and refrigerate for 2 hours.

7. Rinse off the cure and pat dry. Place breasts on a pan rack with linens underneath and leave uncovered in the refrigerator overnight. Fat should be dry to the touch.

8. Place breasts in a cool cast-iron pan on medium-low heat and let render for approximately 15 minutes or until skin has shrunk by at least 2/3. Baste hot fat over the back of breasts until they feel medium rare, approximately 2 minutes. Flip back to skin-side up and place on rack to rest for at least 5 minutes.

9. Slice the duck breasts and serve them with the legs, along with roasted vegetables and a grain of your choosing.

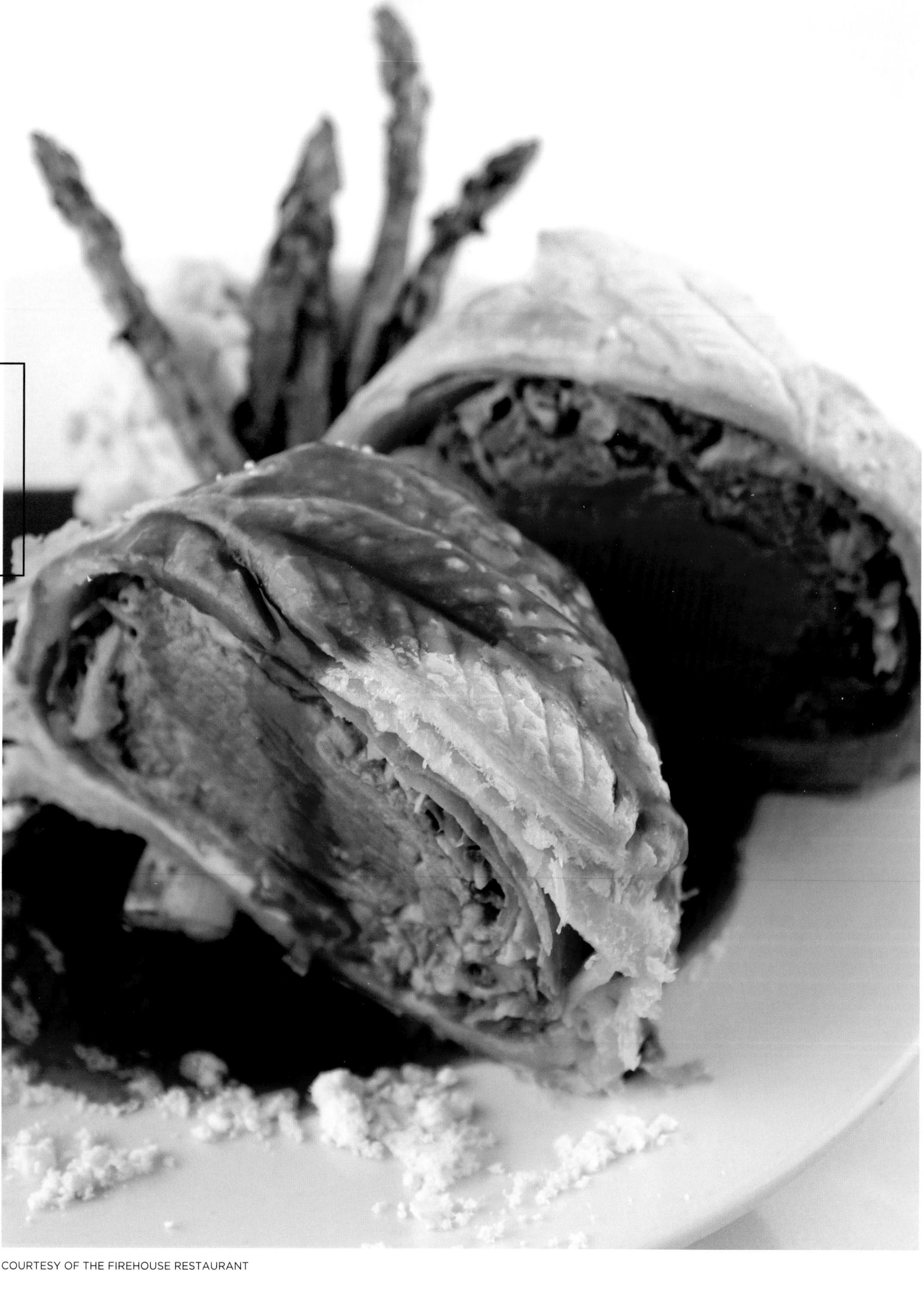

COURTESY OF THE FIREHOUSE RESTAURANT

The Firehouse Restaurant

Beef Wellington

Old Sacramento's finest dining takes place at The Firehouse, the Harvego family's 63-year-old restaurant in a converted fire station. The Firehouse's gorgeous patio, swanky dining room and deep wine cellar have helped it endure the tests of time, as has a commitment to classic American fine dining such as beef Wellington. Steaks wrapped in puff pastry, prosciutto and mushroom duxelles were legendary football coach/broadcaster/video game icon John Madden's go-to dish at his go-to restaurant when passing through Sacramento. While beef Wellington isn't often listed on The Firehouse's menu these days, chef Stephen Ashley can make it upon request, provided customers call at least 48 hours in advance with their number of orders and steak temperature preference.

TIME: AT LEAST 4 1/2 TO 5 1/2 HOURS
SERVES 6

Ingredients

6 8-ounce filet mignon or tenderloin steaks, cut into medallions

1 pound fresh mushrooms (white button, cremini, shiitake, oyster or a combination of these)

2 small shallots, sliced crosswise into rounds

2 large garlic cloves, roughly chopped

2 tablespoons parsley, chopped

4 tablespoons unsalted butter, brought to room temperature

1 teaspoon salt

1/2 teaspoon black pepper

1 cup Dijon mustard

1 pound prosciutto

1/4 cup white flour

14 ounces Dufour Pastry Kitchens puff pastry (1 box)

1 large egg

2–4 teaspoons extra-virgin olive oil

1 tablespoon water

Chef's notes

The thicker the steaks are cut, the better the results will be. Baking time will vary significantly based on the temperature of the Wellingtons when they go in the oven and the cooking style of the oven. The colder the Wellingtons are when they go in the oven, the longer they will need to bake. Convection ovens will also cook Wellingtons much faster than traditional ovens.

Directions

1. Wash steaks and pat them dry. Season them with salt and pepper.

2. Heat 1–2 teaspoons of olive oil in a medium or large cast-iron pan on high heat until it just barely begins to smoke. Sear steaks in the cast-iron pan, approximately 30 seconds per side. Set steaks aside to rest.

3. While the steaks rest, make the mushroom duxelles. Clean and dry the mushrooms. If their sizes vary greatly, cut the larger ones into pieces the size of the smaller ones so all will cook evenly.

4. Heat another 1–2 teaspoons of olive oil in a large saucepan over medium-high heat until warm, then add mushrooms, shallots and garlic. Cook, stirring frequently, until the residual moisture has dissipated and there is little to none visible in the pan, about 4–6 minutes.

continued >

Beef Wellington (continued)

5. Remove the duxelles from heat and immediately stir in the parsley. Transfer the mixture into a bowl and let cool to room temperature.

6. Separate the butter into individual tablespoons. Using a food processor or an immersion blender, pulse the butter and duxelles mixture together to form a very rough paste.

7. Stretch plastic wrap across a medium or large dinner plate. Arrange prosciutto on the plastic wrap in a layer at least as wide as one steak. Add a thin, consistent layer of the mushroom duxelles over the prosciutto.

8. Brush a steak with Dijon mustard until both sides are lightly coated. Place the steak on top of the prosciutto/mushroom duxelles layer (as pictured at right). You may be able to wrap the entire steak with one layer, or a second layer may be needed in order to get full coverage.

9. Once the prosciutto/duxelles layer has been wrapped around the steak, pull the plastic wrap up to create a bag-like pouch. Gather the extra plastic wrap at the top and twist it to create a tight ball around the steak. Repeat the process for all 6 steaks. Secure the twisted tops with a strip of tape and put these plastic-wrapped pouches in the refrigerator for at least 2 hours and up to 24.

10. Heat the oven to 350 degrees. Crack and whisk the egg with water to make an egg wash.

11. Lay out the puff pastry sheet on a large cutting board dusted with flour. Cut into 6 equal-sized portions. The individual pastry squares may need to be flattened slightly with a rolling pin to fully wrap around the steaks.

12. Remove the prosciutto-wrapped steak from its plastic wrap pouch and put it in the middle of the puff pastry square. Brush the interior of the puff pastry not covered by the steak with the egg wash.

98

13. Wrap the puff pastry tightly around the prosciutto-wrapped steak. Brush the exterior of the Wellington with the egg wash.

14. Place a piece of parchment paper in a large sheet pan and lightly coat it with flour. Add the Wellingtons to the pan, spaced at least 1 inch apart from each other.

15. Place the sheet pan in the oven and bake for 20–45 minutes until the puff pastry is golden-brown. Let rest for 5–7 minutes, then halve and serve with your favorite sauce and side dishes. The Firehouse serves its beef Wellingtons with a beef demi-glace, mashed potatoes and asparagus or green beans.

The Firehouse Restaurant
1112 2nd St., Sacramento
(916) 442-4772
firehouseoldsac.com

COURTESY OF THE FIREHOUSE RESTAURANT

Maydoon

Chicken kebabs

Maydoon founder Idean Farid grew up in his father Mohammad's Rancho Cordova restaurant, M. Shahrzad Fine Persian Cuisine, before it was sold in 2020. So shortly after Idean opened his new-school Persian restaurant Maydoon during the pandemic, he turned to Mohammad for help ensuring time-honored dishes would be executed to perfection. The art of preparing and cooking kebabs has been passed down through generations of the Farid family, and their delicious grilled chicken is available on skewers or in rice bowls at the restaurant. This recipe is fairly simple, but will yield big flavors as smoke and spices fill the air.

TIME: 20 MINUTES, PLUS 24–48 HOURS TO MARINATE
SERVES 6

Ingredients

4 pounds chicken thighs

1 large yellow onion, sliced

1 1/4 cup plain yogurt

1/2 cup fresh lime juice

5 garlic cloves, crushed

1/4 cup olive oil

2 tablespoons liquid saffron

4 teaspoons kosher salt

1 teaspoon black pepper

Directions

1. Place the chicken and onion slices in a large container. Combine all other ingredients in a bowl and pour over the chicken. Mix everything thoroughly, cover the container and let marinate for at least 24 hours.

2. Remove chicken from marinade and skewer. Place the skewers on a hot grill and rotate until cooked, about 15–20 minutes. Serve with grilled vegetables and a side of rice.

101

Maydoon
1501 16th St., Suite 111, Sacramento
(916) 382-4309
maydoonrestaurant.com

HECTOR AMEZCUA / THE BEE

Mayahuel

Cochinita pibil

Lobbyists and lovers alike gather at Mayahuel, Ernesto Delgado's Mexican restaurant and tequila museum in the heart of downtown Sacramento. Named in part for Delgado's daughter Maya, it's polished yet inviting, a dignified nod to yesteryear with a lush patio and plenty of vegan options. The menu highlights choice dishes from across Mexico such as cochinita pibil, a pulled pork dish native to the Yucatán Peninsula. Traditionally slow-cooked in a subterranean oven by the Mayans, this indoor version retains its smoky, earthy flavor thanks to the banana leaves, found at most Asian and Mexican supermarkets (and even some general ones).

TIME: ABOUT 3 1/2 HOURS, PLUS AT LEAST 4 HOURS FOR MARINATING
SERVES 4-6

Ingredients

2 1/2 pounds pork shoulder

1 teaspoons ground black pepper

2 tablespoons dried oregano

2 tablespoons white vinegar

1 tablespoons kosher salt

1/2 pound banana leaves

Pickled onions to garnish

Cilantro to garnish

Orange to garnish

Marinade

2 garlic cloves

1 bay leaf

1/2 cup orange juice

1 tablespoons achiote paste

1/4 teaspoon whole cloves

1/4 tablespoon ground black pepper

1/2 cup chicken broth

2 tablespoons white vinegar

3/4 teaspoon kosher salt

A few sprigs of mint

Directions

Make the Marinade

1. In a blender, combine the orange juice, garlic cloves, bay leaf, salt, white vinegar, mint, achiote paste, whole cloves, ground black pepper and chicken broth. Blend until you have a smooth marinade.

2. Place the pork in a bowl or dish and pour the marinade over it, ensuring that the meat is evenly coated. Cover and let it marinate in the refrigerator for at least 4 hours up to overnight.

3. Take the marinated pork out of the refrigerator and allow it to come to room temperature.

Cooking

4. Preheat the oven to 350 degrees. Prepare the banana leaves by briefly heating them over an open flame, making them pliable. Line a heavy Dutch oven or roasting pan with the banana leaves, leaving enough overhang to fold the pork in.

102

Mayahuel
1200 K St., Sacramento
(916) 441-7200
experiencemayahuel.com

HECTOR AMEZCUA / THE BEE

COURTESY OF MAYAHUEL

5. In a small bowl, combine the black pepper, oregano, salt and white vinegar. Pour this mixture over the pork. Place the marinated pork on the banana leaves and fold the leaves over the meat to create a packet. Secure the packet with cooking twine or toothpicks.

6. Cover the Dutch oven or roasting pan with aluminum foil, sealing it tightly. Place the dish in the oven and cook for approximately 2 1/2 to 3 hours, or until the pork is tender and easily pulls apart.

7. Once cooked, remove the dish from the oven and allow it to rest for 10 minutes. Carefully unwrap the banana leaves and transfer the cooked pork to a serving dish. Serve the cochinita pibil with warm tortillas and garnish with toppings such as pickled onions, cilantro and orange slices.

Cousin Jack tacos

Jim "Jimboy" Knudson opened his eponymous taco stand in a Lake Tahoe trailer in 1954, and the Sacramento-area chain remains a family owned nostalgia bomb today as area residents' local alternative to Taco Bell or Del Taco. Pricier restaurants around the city pay homage to Jimboy's iconic ground beef tacos by dusting hard-shell tortillas with Parmesan cheese, and the Knudson family's Cousin Jack tacos are their own gussied-up version of the classic. Named for a lumberjack many years ago, they've been enjoyed on family vacations in the Solomon Islands, the Alaskan wilderness and amid stormy weather on the high seas — but never in an actual Jimboy's.

TIME: 45 MINUTES
YIELDS 10 TACOS

Ingredients

1 pound Monterey Jack cheese, cut into 1/2-inch cubes

2–3 bunches of green onions, chopped into 1/2-inch pieces

1 pound ground beef, 80/20 ratio

10 yellow corn tortillas, 6 inches wide

6–10 cherry tomatoes, cut into 1/2-inch pieces (optional)

1 teaspoon vegetable oil

5 ounces finely grated Parmesan cheese (optional)

Hot sauce to taste (preferably Jimboy's Original Taco Sauce, or Tapatío if not available)

Salt to taste

Black pepper to taste

Directions

Topping

1. Place the Monterey Jack cheese and onions in a medium mixing bowl and mix together with a spoon, turning over carefully. If using tomatoes, leave separate for people to add if they wish. Cover all and set aside.

Meat/tortilla prep

2. Using a butter knife or gloved fingers, spread 1 1/2 ounces of raw ground beef in a thin layer on half of one side of a tortilla, creating a half-moon shape. You want the ground beef to stick to the tortilla. Sprinkle salt and pepper on the meat-covered half, being generous with the seasoning. Repeat this process on up to 10 tortillas and stack them alternately on a tray.

Chef's notes

You can find bottles of Jimboy's Original Taco Sauce at restaurant locations, or via online retailers such as Goldbelly.

Jimboy's Tacos
30+ locations, from Woodland to Cameron Park
jimboystacos.com

LEZLIE STERLING / THE BEE

104

LEZLIE STERLING / THE BEE

Make the tacos

3. Heat an electric skillet to about 400 degrees or large frying pan over medium-high heat. Add the vegetable oil, then place the tortilla on the pan, making sure the meat side is facing up. Move the tortilla slightly around the pan to make sure oil coats its entire bottom.

4. Allow the tortilla to crisp and the meat to begin cooking for 1–2 minutes. Using a spatula, fold the tortilla over the top of the meat, then flip it over so that the other side of the meat will cook through the tortilla, approximately 1 minute. The tortilla should be crispy, and the meat cooked through.

5. Remove the tortilla from the pan and place on a tray or plate. Add a heavy sprinkle of Parmesan cheese to one side of the tortilla, and add toppings (including tomatoes, if using) to the inside of the taco while the taco is hot. Repeat with the remaining prepped tortillas and serve.

Canon

Crispy lamb pavé

Canon burst onto the East Sacramento restaurant scene in 2017, a coolly confident font of endless creativity and pristine execution. Chef/co-owner Brad Cecchi excels at throwing together dishes of which few others could conceive, often (but not always) presented as small bites. This Middle Eastern-inspired lamb entree was named one of The Sacramento Bee's top restaurant dishes of 2018, its tender shredded interior hiding behind a crunchy, toasted shell. It's an intensive creation that requires two different refrigeration periods and several hours of oven time, but the payoff is sure to wow dinner guests.

TIME: OVERNIGHT
SERVES 4-6

Ingredients

4 pounds lamb shoulder, bone-in

1/2 cup Madras curry powder

1/4 cup kosher salt

1 1/2 cups canola oil

1/4 cup harissa paste

Salt to taste

Serve with

1 cup Greek yogurt

30 mint leaves

1 pint pickled giardiniera vegetables

8 pieces flatbread

Directions

1. Combine the salt and curry powder, and rub the mixture over the lamb shoulder to season it. Let marinate in the refrigerator for 4-6 hours.

2. Heat the oven to 300 degrees. Place seasoned lamb in a tight-fitting, oven-safe pot or roasting dish and pour canola oil over it. Cover the pot with its lid or aluminum foil and put it in the oven.

3. Cook for 4-5 hours or until lamb is shreddable. Let cool until you can work with gloved hands. Remove lamb from cooking jus and reserve the liquid for later.

4. Transfer lamb to a bowl and shred by hand, being careful to remove all bones and tendons. Add harissa paste and 4 ounces of cooking jus, then mix. Season with salt to taste.

5. Tightly pack shredded lamb into a 9-inch by 9-inch square baking dish, pressing firmly to ensure there are no bubbles or air pockets. Cover with parchment paper and refrigerate for 8-12 hours or overnight.

6. After the lamb is totally cooled, use a stovetop burner or crème brûlée torch to heat the outside of the baking dish, slightly melting the fat and making it easier to remove the lamb from its mold.

7. Move the lamb onto a cutting board. Cut into desired shape and size (Canon often goes with rectangles).

8. Heat a cast-iron or heavy-bottomed nonstick pan on the stovetop over medium heat. In the dry pan, sear all 4 sides of the lamb slices for 2 minutes each.

9. Remove the lamb from the pan onto a paper towel to absorb excess fat. Serve immediately with yogurt, giardiniera, mint and flatbread.

107

Canon
1719 34th St., Sacramento
(916) 469-2433
canoneastsac.com

LEZLIE STERLING / THE BEE

Saigon Alley Kitchen & Bar

Garlic noodles

Vietnamese food is one of Sacramento's culinary strengths, but hadn't really been transformed through a modern, bright lens before Mymy Nguyen-Vong and Jimmy Voong opened Saigon Alley in midtown at the start of 2020. Centered around a tapas-style happy hour and sterling cocktail bar, it's a great first date spot for inventive bites rooted in the flavors of Stockton Boulevard. Nguyen also opened a Saigon Alley in North Natomas in June 2023, along with Sit Lo Saigon restaurants in Elk Grove and Davis. This noodle dish is packed with umami between the oyster and fish sauces, garlic and Parmesan cheese, yet simple enough to become a weeknight staple.

TIME: 20 MINUTES
SERVES 1

Ingredients

1 cup uncooked egg noodles

1 garlic clove, minced

1 1/2 teaspoons oyster sauce

1 teaspoon sugar

1 teaspoon fish sauce

1 1/2 teaspoons water, plus more for cooking noodles

1 tablespoon butter

2 tablespoons Parmesan cheese, grated

1 tablespoon scallions, chopped

1 cilantro sprig to garnish

Directions

1. Fill a large pot with water. Bring to a boil and cook the egg noodles according to their package instructions. Once cooked, drain the noodles and set them aside.

2. Mix the garlic, oyster sauce, sugar, fish sauce and 1 1/2 teaspoons water in a small bowl. Stir well to combine.

3. Heat a large skillet or wok over medium-high heat. Add the butter to the skillet and let it melt. Add the cooked egg noodles to the skillet and stir-fry for about 2 minutes, coating them evenly with the melted butter.

4. Pour the prepared garlic sauce over the stir-fried noodles in the skillet. Continue to stir-fry for another 2 minutes, ensuring that the noodles are well-coated with the sauce.

5. Transfer the garlic noodles to a serving plate. Sprinkle Parmesan cheese evenly over the noodles, then top with scallions. Place a sprig of cilantro on the side as a garnish. Serve hot.

108

Saigon Alley Kitchen & Bar
1801 L St., Suite 50, Sacramento
(916) 758-6934
4630 Natomas Blvd., Suite 150, Sacramento
(916) 515-8184
saigonalley.com

KEVIN NERI / THE BEE

Skip's Kitchen

Hamburger

All-American food, done well. That's the ethos behind Skip's Kitchen, a burger den that's become one of Carmichael's most-frequented restaurants since opening in 2011. This classic burger is considered one of the best around and still sells for less than $12, though it's even cheaper to grill your own. Juicy and messy, it's what put Skip's on the map and kept it around, according to owner Skip Wahl. Although Wahl isn't ready to divulge the spices beyond smoked paprika that make Skip's burgers shine, other burger chefs commonly deploy some combination of salt, black pepper, onion powder and garlic powder.

TIME: 25 MINUTES
SERVES 1

Ingredients

8 ounces of 85% lean ground beef (chuck/sirloin blend preferred)

1 brioche bun

1 tablespoon ketchup

1 tablespoon mayonnaise

1/2 tablespoon whole grain mustard

1/2 tablespoon butter

1 slice tomato

1 slice red onion

1 ounce lettuce, shredded (iceberg preferred)

3 dill pickle chips

Spice blend of your choosing

Directions

1. Season both sides of meat with your spice blend — Skip's includes smoked paprika, along with five other secret ingredients. Form the meat into a ball and refrigerate. Mix the ketchup, mayonnaise and mustard to create Skip's house sauce, then set aside.

2. Heat the grill to medium-high. Butter the brioche bun and toast on the grill until golden-brown. Layer half the house sauce on the bottom bun along with the pickles, lettuce, onion and tomato slice.

3. Smash the patty onto the grill, flattening it somewhat, and add more seasoning to the side facing up. Cook for 4 minutes, then flip the patty and season the patty's other side. Remove after 4 more minutes and place on the dressed bottom bun.

4. Spread the other half of the house sauce on the top bun, then place atop the patty.

Chef's notes

Skip's serves its burgers with sweet potato or waffle fries; do so at home for the full experience. The restaurant also offers this burger — all burgers, in fact — with a housemade walnut/mushroom patty as a vegetarian option.

Skip's Kitchen
4717 El Camino Ave., Carmichael
(916) 514-0830
skipskitchen.com

KEVIN NERI / THE BEE

Hot and spicy lemongrass chicken (gà xào sả ỡt)

Mai Pham was born in Vietnam, grew up in Thailand, then made both countries' cuisines her livelihood when she opened Lemon Grass in 1989. The Arden Arcade restaurant became a local favorite as Pham ascended to the national spotlight, hosting "Vietnam: My Country, My Kitchen" on the Food Network and writing a James Beard Award-finalist cookbook. People still flock to Pham and partner Tyler Bond's restaurant for dishes such as this Vietnamese hot and spicy lemongrass chicken, which can also be made with pork or eel. Whatever protein you choose, be sure to use a very hot pan and add the appropriate amount of onions, lemongrass and chiles.

TIME: 30 MINUTES
SERVES 4

Ingredients

2 tablespoons sugar

1/4 cup hot water

3 tablespoons vegetable oil

1 1/2 cups yellow onions, cut into 1/4-inch slices

1 tablespoon garlic, minced

2/3 lb boneless, skinless chicken thighs, cut into bite-sized strips 1 inch by 2 1/2-inches thick

2 teaspoons chopped red chiles, Thai chiles or red Fresno chiles, or to taste

1/2 tablespoon chili flakes, or to taste

4 tablespoons lemongrass, minced

1/2 teaspoon sea salt

1 tablespoon fish sauce

1/4 cup light chicken stock or water

2 to 3 tablespoons slurry (1 tablespoon cornstarch + 4 tablespoons water)

10 cilantro sprigs, cut into 1/2-inch lengths to garnish

Directions

1. To make the caramel sauce, place sugar in a pan over medium heat. Allow to cook undisturbed for 1 minute until the sugar melts and turns dark brown. Carefully (it will splatter a bit) add hot water to stop the cooking. Set this aside.

2. Heat another stir-fry pan (preferably nonstick) over medium until very hot. Add the vegetable oil, onions and garlic and stir until fragrant, about 1 minute. Add the chicken, chiles, lemongrass, salt and fish sauce. Stir and cook for about 3 minutes. Reduce heat to medium, then add the caramel sauce and chicken stock or water. Cover and simmer until chicken is done, another 3–5 minutes.

3. Stir in the slurry 1 tablespoon at a time, just enough to slightly thicken the sauce and coat the chicken. Transfer to your serving dish, garnish with cilantro and additional chiles if you like, and serve immediately with rice.

Lemon Grass Restaurant
601 Munroe St., Sacramento
(916) 486-4891
lemongrassrestaurant.com

COURTESY OF LEMON GRASS RESTAURANT

114

Frank Fat's

Immigrant's beef

Frank Fat immigrated from China in 1919 and established his namesake restaurant in downtown Sacramento 20 years later. It grew to be a preferred hidey-hole of lobbyists and politicians: former Gov. Jerry Brown was known to eat with the cooks after hours during his first term, and longtime California Assembly Speaker Willie Brown famously sketched out an 11th-hour deal on a Frank Fat's cloth napkin. But it was Fat's daughter-in-law Lina, a Hong Kong native, who carried Fat Family Restaurant Group into the late 20th and early 21st centuries. A pharmacist by trade, Lina Fat helped create the recipe for immigrant's beef at China Camp, one of the family's former restaurants in Old Sacramento. In her 1992 project "The Lina Fat Cookbook: Recipes from the Fat Family Restaurants," the late chef called it a typical Chinese immigrant dish for its use of traditional seasonings to flavor the available meat and vegetables. It was selected for this cookbook by Lina Fat's son Kevin, the restaurant group's current CEO/operating partner.

TIME: 25–35 MINUTES, PLUS AT LEAST 2 HOURS OF MARINATING
SERVES 4

Ingredients

1 large (1 1/2 to 2 pounds) flank steak

24 trimmed asparagus spears
or 4-6 broccoli spears

1/4 cup soy sauce

1/4 cup vegetable oil

1 tablespoon brandy

1 tablespoon garlic, minced

1 tablespoon fresh ginger, minced

1/4 teaspoon sesame oil

1 tablespoon olive or corn oil

2 teaspoons cornstarch

2 tablespoons kosher salt

Directions

1. Trim fat from the flank steak. Cut meat lengthwise into 3-inch wide strips; cut diagonally across the grain to make 2-inch wide pieces. When cutting, hold the knife at an angle so each piece of meat is about 1/4-inch thick.

2. In a medium bowl, combine soy sauce, vegetable oil, brandy, garlic, ginger, sesame oil and cornstarch. Add beef and stir to coat. Cover and refrigerate for at least 2 hours or overnight.

3. Fill a pot with 8 cups of water, bring it to a boil and add kosher salt. Blanch asparagus or broccoli in boiling salted water for 3–5 minutes or until barely tender. Drain, rinse with cold water and drain again. Arrange on a serving platter.

4. Heat a wide, heavy frying pan over high heat and grease lightly with olive or corn oil. Cook meat in pan, turning once, until brown on both sides, about 3-4 minutes total. Arrange meat over blanched asparagus or broccoli and serve.

115

Chef's notes

Fresh ginger should have a thin skin that's neither wrinkled nor dry, Lina Fat wrote. To mince here, she recommended smashing slices of unpeeled ginger with the flat side of a cleaver or chef's knife, then chopping them very finely.

Frank Fat's
806 L St., Sacramento
(916) 442-7092
frankfats.com

PAUL KITAGAKI JR. / THE BEE

Chicha Peruvian Kitchen & Cafe

Lomo saltado

Once considered the land of chain restaurants, Roseville's dining scene has grown in leaps and bounds over the last five years along with its population. One of the dining scene's new stars is Chicha, Giancarlo Zapata and Marleny Chávez's ode to their native Peru. Peruvian food often represents the cultural criss-crossing that's shaped the South American nation since colonial times, and the ever-popular lomo saltado is a shining example. Chinese Peruvian laborers contributed soy sauce, stir-frying and the rice served alongside this beef-and-potatoes dish, making it one of the ultimate "Chifa" dishes.

TIME: 25 MINUTES
SERVES 2

Ingredients

12 ounces beef tenderloin

1 medium red onion

1 large tomato

1 Peruvian yellow chile pepper (aji amarillo), or more for added spice

4 tablespoons canola oil

2 garlic cloves, minced

1 ounce red wine vinegar

3 ounces light soy sauce

2 eggs

2 tablespoons cilantro, finely chopped

Salt to taste

Cumin to taste

Directions

1. Cut the beef tenderloin into medium-sized rectangular pieces, about 1 1/2 inches each. Salt and cumin the meat to taste.

2. Cut the red onion and tomato into 8 pieces each. Cut the aji amarillo into thin julienne strips.

3. Heat 3 tablespoons of canola oil in a skillet over very high heat. Add the beef and toss in the oil.

4. When the meat begins to brown, about 4–5 minutes, add the onion and garlic. Let them cook for a few more minutes until they become crispy. Add the aji amarillo and cook for another 3 minutes.

5. Add the tomato and cook for about 2 minutes. Add the red wine vinegar and let cook for 1 more minute. Add the soy sauce, stir well, remove from heat and plate.

6. Heat 1 tablespoon of canola oil in a medium-sized pan over medium heat. Crack eggs into pan, fry to preferred doneness and set atop beef. Sprinkle the chopped cilantro over everything.

Chef's notes

Runny egg yolks will create a wonderfully gooey mess. Soak it up with a side of steamed rice or about 6 ounces of french fries.

116

HECTOR AMEZCUA / THE BEE

Chicha Peruvian Kitchen & Cafe
1079 Sunrise Ave., Suite O, Roseville
(916) 666-7998
peruvianrestaurantroseville.com

Urban Roots Brewery & Smokehouse

Smoked spare ribs

When Greg Desmangles thinks about the barbecue he grew up on, he remembers his dad serving ribs at summer pool parties in the northern Sacramento County suburb of Antelope. Now the culinary director over Urban Roots as well as fried chicken haven Bawk and globally inspired Pangaea Bier Cafe, Desmangles captures that childhood sense of nostalgia in these smoked spare ribs. Cooked low and slow, they're one of the star items at the craft brewery and barbecue joint in Southside Park just south of downtown Sacramento. Pick your favorite premade barbecue sauce to make the "mop sauce," a vinegary blend used to baste the meat as it cooks.

TIME: 5–6 HOURS
SERVES 6

Ingredients

1 rack spare ribs

1/4 cup yellow mustard

2 cups barbecue sauce

2 cups apple cider vinegar, plus more in a spray bottle

Rub

2 cups kosher salt

1 1/2 cups brown sugar

1 1/2 cups black pepper

1/4 cup ground ginger

1/4 cup paprika

Chef's notes

Resist the urge to check on the ribs during the first 3 hours. Heat escapes every time you do so, prolonging the cooking process.

Directions

1. Preheat smoker to 250 degrees. Combine all ingredients for the rub in a bowl, mixing well.

2. Remove the sternum bone from the spare ribs. Trim the flap or any thin meat from the edges of the ribs. Flip the rack over and use a paper towel to remove the connective tissue covering the ribs.

3. Slather a thin layer of yellow mustard across the ribs. Sprinkle the rub onto the ribs from about 1 foot above, using your hand or a seasoning shaker. Be sure to season evenly so there are no gaps on either side of the ribs. Place the ribs in the smoker and let cook for at least 3 hours.

4. While the ribs are cooking, create the mop sauce by combining the barbecue sauce and apple cider vinegar in a mixing bowl.

5. Check the ribs after 3 hours; they should have developed a reddish-brown hue. Mist the ribs with apple cider vinegar using the spray bottle, and repeat this process every 30 minutes for the next hour.

6. After 4 hours of total cooking time, apply the first layer of mop sauce. Re-apply mop every 30 minutes for the next hour or until the ribs are done.

7. When the ribs have reached an internal temperature of 195 degrees, mop them one last time. Wrap the ribs in foil and rest them meat-side down for about 30 minutes.

8. Slice the ribs into individual pieces and enjoy. Desmangles recommends serving your ribs with coleslaw, potato salad and/or baked beans.

Urban Roots Brewery & Smokehouse

1322 V St., Sacramento
(916) 706-3741
urbanrootsbrewing.com

RENÉE C. BYER / THE BEE

Camden Spit & Larder

Steak and ale pie

Oliver Ridgeway's native England meets California freshness at Camden Spit & Larder, his Capital Mall brasserie that opened in 2018. Named for Ridgeway's son as well as a bustling London neighborhood, Camden is affably high-end, an easy choice for a business lunch that also draws Kings fans for pregame happy hours. Though Camden does make individual steak and ale pies as an appetizer, this is a recipe for one large shareable pie, which Ridgeway recommends pairing with mashed potatoes, steak fries or seasonal vegetables.

TIME: 1 1/2 TO 2 HOURS
SERVES 6–8

Ingredients

For the pastry

3 cups all-purpose flour

1/2 teaspoon salt

2 sticks unsalted butter, cubed and kept cold until ready to use

1/2 cup cold water

1 large egg, beaten to brush on pastry

For the filling

2 tablespoons vegetable oil

2 pounds beef chuck roast or shoulder, cut into 1/2-inch cubes

1 medium onion, chopped

2 medium carrots, cut into bite-sized chunks

2 garlic cloves, finely chopped

2 tablespoons tomato paste

2 tablespoons Worcestershire sauce

2 tablespoons all-purpose flour

3/4 cup dark English ale or local IPA

1/2 cup beef stock (reduced sodium if possible)

1/2 teaspoon fresh thyme, finely chopped

1/2 teaspoon fresh rosemary, finely chopped

1 teaspoon salt

1/4 teaspoon ground black pepper

1 large egg, beaten

1 bag dried beans (optional)

Directions

To make the pastry by hand

1. Add the flour, salt and butter to a large bowl. Using your fingertips or a pastry cutter, rub the butter and flour until it resembles breadcrumbs. Drizzle in the water and mix using a fork until the solution holds together when pressed in your hand. Remove and shape into a ball on a floured board. Cover in plastic wrap and refrigerate.

Make the filling

2. Add the vegetable oil to a large, heavy, ovenproof saucepan or braising pan over medium high heat. Add the beef (working in batches so as to not overcrowd the pan) and cook, turning the pieces until brown on all sides. When all pieces are browned, remove and set aside.

3. Add onions and carrots to the same pan and cook until onions soften, about 5 minutes. Add garlic, tomato paste and Worcestershire sauce. Stir to mix well and cook for 1 minute.

4. Sprinkle in the flour and stir well until all the flour is well-mixed. Cook for 2 minutes, then add the ale and stir until it starts to thicken. Stir in the beef stock, thyme, rosemary and salt, then cover with a lid and allow to come to a low simmer for 1 hour (time will depend on the size of the beef pieces). Remove the lid and simmer for 15 more minutes to thicken the liquid if needed — it should not be runny. The meat should be quite tender, but will also continue cooking in the oven.

120

continued >

Steak and ale pie (continued)

5.   Preheat the oven to 425 degrees with the rack in the center. Lightly butter a 9- or 10-inch pie dish.

6.   Remove the dough from the refrigerator and cut in half. Place one half back in the plastic wrap and refrigerate. Roll out the other half onto a floured surface to a thickness of 1/8-inch. Cut a circle from the dough 1/2-inch larger than your pan and place into the pie dish, allowing the edge to hang over.

7.   Cut a large circle of parchment paper or foil larger than the pan and place on top of the pastry in the pie dish. Pour the dried beans to the center to weigh down the dough, or place a piece of foil on top of the dough and weigh down with an oven-proof dish that will fit inside.

8.   Bake for 12 minutes until you start to see the edges get a little golden-brown. Remove the crust from the oven, grab the corners of the paper or foil and remove the beans. If it puffs, it should go down. Return the crust to the oven for 5 more minutes to cook the pastry.

9.   Once the crust is out of the oven, take the rest of the dough, roll out onto a floured surface and cut a 10-inch circle. Fill the cooked crust with the beef filling.

10.   Brush the edges of the uncooked pastry with the beaten egg. Roll the pastry circle over the rolling pin, lift and place on top of the pie with the egg-washed edges down so they stick to the other dough, folding the edge of the top dough under the bottom dough and pinch to seal, or press with a fork.

11.   Brush the entire top with egg wash and cut a couple of slits in the center of the crust. Bake for about 25 minutes until golden-brown. Remove from oven and let rest for 10 minutes to allow the sauce to thicken, then slice and serve.

Camden Spit & Larder
555 Capitol Mall, Suite 100, Sacramento
(916) 619-8897
camdenspitandlarder.com

PAUL KITAGAKI JR. / THE BEE

123

Sushi Q

Steamed sea bass

Here's what you need to know about Sushi Q: Qui and Kim Tu's Japanese restaurant is possibly Sacramento's best family friendly sushi spot, but it's not yet a household name outside of Elk Grove and South Land Park. The cuts are immaculate, the atmosphere is convivial and the prices are reasonable. The steamed sea bass entree, available at market price in both restaurants, is similarly straightforward enough to make at home. Best accompanied by a bowl of white rice, it's melt-in-your-mouth tender when done right.

TIME: 20 MINUTES
SERVES 1

Ingredients

8-ounce Chilean sea bass filet

2 green onions

1 ounce cilantro (preferably micro cilantro)

1 ounce fresh ginger, skin peeled

2 tablespoons light sesame oil

3 tablespoons low sodium soy sauce

1 teaspoon sugar or honey

1 lemon wedge

Pinch of dashi powder (about 1/4 gram)

Directions

1. Rinse the sea bass and pat dry. Grind ginger finely and spread it on top of the sea bass.

2. Fill a steamer halfway with water and bring it to a boil. Place the sea bass in the steamer basket and cook for about 12 minutes, ensuring that the filet's center temperature reaches 145 degrees.

3. While sea bass is cooking, slice the green onions and cilantro into long strips and place them into an ice bath for 5 minutes. Take the vegetables out and place them on top of a paper towel.

4. Mix soy sauce, sugar/honey and dashi powder together in a small mixing bowl until diluted.

5. When the sea bass is cooked, place it in the center of a serving plate and sprinkle half of the green onion/cilantro mix on top. Heat the sesame oil in a small pan until it begins to smoke, about 1 1/2 to 2 minutes.

6. Pour the hot sesame oil over the sea bass. Do the same with the soy sauce mixture, then garnish with the remaining green onion/cilantro mix to your liking. Squeeze the lemon wedge over the dish and serve with white rice.

125

Sushi Q
1339 Florin Road, Suite B101, Sacramento
(916) 942-9225
8325 Elk Grove Florin Road, Suite 400, Sacramento
(916) 896-0116
sushiq916.com

BENJY EGEL / THE BEE

Desserts

127

Freeport Bakery

Almond horns

The son of Bavarian bakers was finishing a cross-country motorcycle trip when he walked into a San Diego bookstore and met his future wife, a Chicago transplant who happened to be seeking German language lessons. Thus goes the meet-cute story of Marlene and Walter Goetzeler, who moved north and turned Freeport Bakery into a Sacramento institution in 1987. Office parties and birthdays have been brightened by the presence of Freeport's pink boxes over the last three-and-a-half decades, and the Goetzelers' Land Park bakery has grown to need a neighboring commercial kitchen. These chocolate-dipped almond horns can be found in Freeport's display case, or in happy homes across the region.

TIME: 40 MINUTES
SERVES APPROXIMATELY 16 PASTRIES

Ingredients

1 pound almond paste

7 ounces granulated sugar

1/3 cup egg whites

1 cup sliced almonds

8 ounces dark chocolate

Directions

1. Preheat the oven to 320 degrees. Break up the almond paste in a mixer, adding small amounts of egg whites to help it come apart.

2. Add sugar slowly. If the mixture is too stiff, keep adding egg whites. You want it to be about the consistency of Play-Doh.

3. Spread the sliced almonds on a sheet pan. Scoop balls of the mixture, approximately 3 inches long and thicker in the middle than the ends, onto the almonds using a tablespoon. Roll each ball gently in the almonds.

4. Place balls on a papered sheet pan. Shape into wide "U" shapes, forming horns. Place the horns in the oven and bake until light golden-brown, about 20 minutes. Remove and let cool.

5. Meanwhile, melt the dark chocolate in a double boiler. Dip almond horn ends into melted chocolate.

6. Serve and enjoy. Almond horns can be stored in airtight containers for up to one week, or frozen for later enjoyment.

129

Freeport Bakery
2966 Freeport Blvd., Sacramento
(916) 442-4256
freeportbakery.com

KEVIN NERI / THE BEE

Ginger Elizabeth

Chocolate molten soufflé cakes

Ginger Elizabeth Hahn grew up in the heart of Apple Hill, a network of orchards and wineries an hour east of Sacramento in El Dorado County. She fell in love with fruit at a young age, and her J Street pâtisserie regularly extracts brilliance from local growers' passion fruit or oranges. Yet Hahn made her name in chocolate, opening her first confectionery in midtown's Handle District in 2008 after crafting desserts in New York, Chicago and El Dorado Hills. The J Street pâtisserie followed in 2020, then Hahn combined both stores in 2023, much as these molten soufflé cakes combine her pastry and chocolate prowess. They're designed to be baked in 4-ounce ramekins, and should hold firm on the edges without compromising the liquid center.

TIME: 25–35 MINUTES
SERVES 8–10 IN 4-OUNCE RAMEKINS

Ingredients

2 sticks unsalted butter

1 1/4 cup Ginger Elizabeth Classic Hot Chocolate Mix or 52–58% cacao chocolate mix

2 1/4 cups powdered sugar, sifted

5 egg yolks

5 whole eggs

1 cup all-purpose flour, sifted

1/2 teaspoon salt

1 teaspoon vanilla extract

130

Chef's notes

Enjoy these cakes warm with a scoop of toasted coconut or mint ice cream, and top it off with some Ginger Elizabeth Chocolate Fudge Sauce (available at the pâtisserie or online) to complete your sundae.

Directions

1. Preheat the oven to 375 degrees. Heavily spray ramekins with cooking spray and set aside.

2. Melt the butter and chocolate over a double boiler on medium heat. After the butter and chocolate are melted to 130 degrees, remove the bowl from the double boiler and wipe the water from the bottom.

3. By hand or machine, whisk in the powdered sugar until the mixture is homogeneous. Add the egg yolks, whisk in, scrape and whisk again. Add the eggs and vanilla extract to the chocolate mixture and mix until combined.

4. Add the all-purpose flour and salt. Whisk in gently until it is just combined and no lumps of flour remain.

5. Scoop and fill the batter into the prepared ramekins about 1/2-inch from the top. Bake for 8–10 minutes. The cakes should be firm for a half-inch around the edges, but liquid in the center. Let cool for 3–5 minutes and unmold.

Ginger Elizabeth
2413 J St., Suite 120, Sacramento
(916) 706-1738
gingerelizabeth.com

PAUL KITAGAKI JR. / THE BEE

COURTESY OF GINGER ELIZABETH

Faria Bakery

Fig leaf and jam rye sheet cake

Chris Beattie founded Faria as a cottage bakery after moving to Sacramento, but his naturally leavened breads couldn't be limited to farmers markets and pop-ups. The main bakery in Oak Park, a rapidly changing neighborhood southeast of Sacramento's urban core, opened to rave reviews in 2019 and was followed by a Folsom Historic District shop a half-hour east in 2022. Pastry chef Natalie Quach has helped Sacramento's hottest bread bakery build out its repertoire of sweets with ingenious, locally sourced creations such as this fruit-and-rye cake, which can be tweaked based on what's in your backyard. Use lemon verbena or basil instead of fig leaves, for example, and decorate the top of the cake to your artistic preference.

TIME: AT LEAST 2 HOURS
SERVES 12–16

Ingredients

Rye cake

2 sticks butter

2 1/2 cups granulated sugar

1/2 cup plus 2 tablespoons brown sugar

5 eggs, room temperature

3/4 cup plus 2 1/3 tablespoons buttermilk, room temperature

2/3 cup neutral oil

1 2/3 tablespoons vanilla

3 2/3 cups medium rye flour

1/2 tablespoon baking powder

2/3 teaspoon salt

1 cup simple syrup (1:1 sugar-to-water ratio) or other cake soak

Jam

9 ounces of your favorite jam or:

1 cup of dark fruit such as blueberries, blackberries, cherries or mulberries

1/2 cup sugar

1/3 tablespoon lemon juice

Fig leaf Swiss buttercream

2 cups fig leaves

3/4 cup neutral oil

2/3 cup egg whites, about 5 or 6 eggs

1 1/2 cups sugar

1/4 teaspoon cream of tartar

5 sticks butter, room temperature

Chef's notes

Every component in this recipe can be made ahead of time. Freeze the cake for up to 3 weeks. Uncanned jam will keep in the fridge for up to 3 weeks. The oil will hold for up to 2 weeks once made. Even the buttercream can be stored in the fridge for 2 weeks, or frozen for a month.

Directions

Jam

1. Place a small plate or saucer in the freezer. Purée your chosen fruit. In a saucepan, combine the fruit solution with sugar and lemon juice. Cook on medium-high heat until very thick and boiling, about 20–30 minutes.

2. When you suspect the jam is finished, remove the plate and place a dollop of jam in the center. Return to the freezer for 2 minutes, then remove again and test with your finger. If the jam wrinkles and feels gel-like, it's ready to be removed; if not, cook a little while longer. When done cooking, pour the jam into a separate container to cool and keep in the fridge until ready to use.

Rye cake

3. Preheat the oven to 350 degrees. Lightly spray a half-sheet pan and line it with parchment paper. Combine buttermilk, oil and vanilla in a pourable container. Whisk the rye flour, baking powder and salt together in a separate bowl.

4. Cream the butter, granulated sugar and brown sugar with the beaters on medium to medium-high until light and fluffy, about 6–8 minutes. Slowly add in the eggs, one at a time, waiting until the last egg is fully incorporated before adding the next one. Stop the mixer and scrape down the sides of the bowl with a flexible spatula to bring up uncreamed butter, sugar and eggs. Continue creaming until light and fluffy again.

133

continued >

Fig leaf and jam rye sheet cake (continued)

5.   Reduce speed to low and slowly stream in the liquids, making sure that the stream is never wider than a pencil. Increase speed to medium and continue creaming until light and fluffy, about 5–6 minutes. Stop the mixer and scrape down the sides, then cream for 2–3 minutes more.

6.   Reduce speed on mixer to low and slowly incorporate the dry ingredients. Stop just as soon as they are combined. Scrape down the sides and gently incorporate any pockets of remaining flour. Pour the batter into a prepared pan and smooth the top with a spatula. Bake for 30 minutes, or until a toothpick or knife can go into the cake and come out clean. Set aside to cool and, if preparing for later use, wrap with plastic wrap and freeze. If making the cake today, it can be frozen without wrapping.

Fig leaf oil

7.   Prepare a bowl of ice water and bring a pot of water to boil. Submerge fig leaves in the boiling water for 30–60 seconds until bright green. Quickly remove leaves and immediately dunk into ice water to halt cooking. Once chilled, lay leaves onto a towel and pat dry.

8.   Blend the fig leaves and oil in a high-speed blender until completely smooth. If necessary, add more oil to help the blender along.

9.   Line a sieve or funnel with extremely fine cheesecloth or a coffee filter. Place over a bowl. Pour the mixture into the filter and let it sit overnight, stirring occasionally. The oil should be green and pure in the morning. Store in the refrigerator for up to one week or freeze for up to one month.

134

Swiss buttercream

10.   Combine the egg whites, sugar and cream of tartar in a stand mixer bowl and cook in a bain-marie (double boiler) until the mixture reaches 185 degrees. Make sure to whisk frequently. Once the egg whites reach temperature, immediately transfer to the stand mixer and begin whisking on high. Whisk until the bowl is cool to the touch, about 15 minutes.

11.   Add the room temperature butter in pats, going slowly to avoid breaking the buttercream. Once everything is incorporated, reduce speed to medium and slowly stream in the fig oil until the desired flavor is achieved. Use the paddle attachment to smooth out any large bubbles. Buttercream is ready to use immediately, or store in the fridge or freezer until ready.

Faria Bakery
3417 Broadway, Sacramento
(916) 204-8726
604 Sutter St., Folsom
(916) 906-5841
fariabakery.com

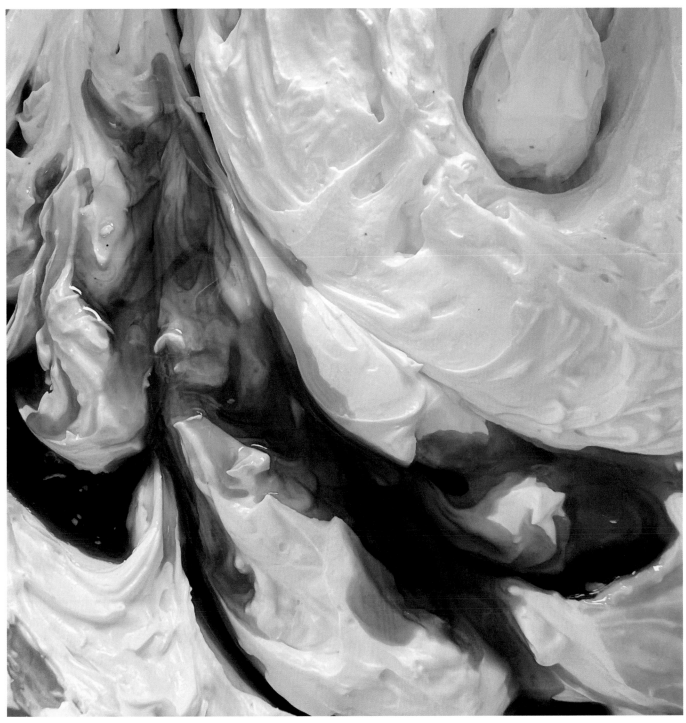

COURTESY OF FARIA BAKERY

Assembly

12. Cut the cake in half widthwise (think hamburger, not hot dog). On one piece of cake (which will be the bottom), brush simple syrup or any desired cake soaker to increase moisture. Pipe a 1/2-inch border around the edges with the buttercream. Fill the inside of this border with jam. Lay the top layer of the cake on this.

13. Roughly coat the entire cake with a thin layer of buttercream. Smooth it all out with an offset spatula, creating the crumb coat. Chill the cake in the fridge or freezer for 30 minutes. Remove the cake and continue frosting until the sides and top are smooth and well-covered.

14. Finally, the fun part. Decorate the top however you like! Faria likes to use fresh fruit and get creative with piping techniques. Pools of jam, edible flowers and powdered herbs are always a nice touch.

Estelle Bakery & Pâtisserie

Lavender shortbread

Bay Area native Esther Son's path to school often included a stop at a local bakery, and lunchtime was known to feature madeleines in lieu of sandwiches. It's little surprise, then, that Son opened her French-inspired bakery in 2011, which grew its following on the back of classic European pastries and delightful tartines. Estelle's original location closed in 2016, but she established the bakery's current headquarters in the northeastern Sacramento neighborhood of Arden Arcade a year later, then added a pint-sized shop in Downtown Commons by the Kings' arena (a Davis location is in progress as of this writing). This lavender shortbread is a charming, elegant dessert for those seeking a tea companion more so than a sugar bomb.

TIME: 25–30 MINUTES
SERVES APPROXIMATELY 24 PASTRIES

Ingredients

1 stick unsalted butter, softened

1/3 cup granulated sugar

1/4 teaspoon salt

1/4 teaspoon vanilla

1 1/4 cups all-purpose flour

1 to 2 teaspoons dried lavender buds, crushed

Coarse sugar to garnish (optional)

Directions

1. In a large mixing bowl, beat the butter with an electric mixer on medium to high speed for 30 seconds. Add granulated sugar, salt and vanilla. Beat until combined, scraping sides of bowl occasionally. Beat in the flour (mixture will be crumbly). Stir in lavender. Using your hands, form the flour mixture into a ball and knead until smooth.

2. Preheat the oven to 325 degrees. On a lightly floured surface, roll dough to about 3/8 of an inch thick. Cut cookies using a 2- to 3-inch cookie cutter (Estelle uses a flower shape).

3. Place cookies 1 inch apart on ungreased cookie sheets. Sprinkle with coarse sugar if desired. Re-roll dough as needed.

4. Place cookies in the oven and bake for 8 minutes. Rotate cookie sheet front to back. Bake for 5 to 6 more minutes or until the edges are firm and lightly browned. Transfer cookies to a wire rack and cool completely.

5. To store, layer cookies between waxed paper in an airtight container. Store at room temperature for up to 3 days or freeze for up to 3 months.

Estelle Bakery & Pâtisserie
2530 Arden Way, Sacramento and
615 David J. Stern Walk, Suite 100, Sacramento
(916) 551-1500
estellebakery.com

KEVIN NERI / THE BEE

Yume Gelato

Strawberry-basil ice pops or sorbet

Mike Janwar and Lucy Xu tested recipes at home for a year before opening Yume Gelato, their East Sacramento gelateria, in 2019. Across Folsom Boulevard from iconic gourmet grocer Corti Brothers and a smattering of restaurants, it's become a go-to place for cold treats, with strong gluten- and dairy-free selections. The Asian American owners frequently play with ingredients such as pandan or black sesame, but focus primarily on what flavors will go best together, such as this lovely strawberry-basil concoction. The same recipe can be used for ice pops or sorbet; the method of freezing is the only difference.

TIME: 20–30 MINUTES FOR PREP AND BLENDING, THEN 4–10 HOURS OF FREEZING FOR ICE POPS
OR 30–45 MINUTES OF CHURNING FOR SORBET
SERVES ABOUT 10 ICE POPS (3 1/2 OUNCES EACH) OR 8–9 BOWLS OF SORBET

138

Ingredients

1 pound plus 1 1/2 ounces strawberries

1 1/8 cups water (filtered preferred)

1 1/8 cups granulated cane sugar

1/2 ounce lemon juice

3–4 basil leaves

Directions

1. If using frozen strawberries, defrost them overnight in the fridge before using. For fresh strawberries, wash them under cold water and remove the leaves.

2. Quarter the strawberries. Wash the basil leaves under cold water and set them aside.

3. Place the strawberries, sugar and lemon juice in the blender and set it to the highest speed to blend them well, about 3–5 minutes. The texture should resemble a strawberry smoothie when done.

4. Add the basil leaves to the blender and set it to a low speed (if your blender has a 1–10 speed scale, set it to 3) for 5–10 seconds.

5. Strain the whole strawberry-basil mixture through a mesh strainer to remove the strawberry seeds and basil leaves.

6. If making ice pops, pour the mixture into ice pop molds, add ice pop sticks and leave them in the freezer overnight. It may take anywhere from 4–10 hours for the ice pops to properly freeze depending on the size of the mold and freezer temperature.

7. If making sorbet, set the ice cream maker to its setting (if applicable) or churn for 30–45 minutes if not (time may vary based on type of machine). You want to get the texture of a frozen, dense slushy that's not watery. When the machine is done churning, you can remove the sorbet and enjoy it immediately, or freeze it for later use.

Yume Gelato
5921 Folsom Blvd., Sacramento
(916) 400-4062
instagram.com/yumegelato

BENJY EGEL / THE BEE

Cocktails

141

The Butterscotch Den

Freezer martini

Oak Park's hottest bar is Irish Hospitality Group's newest outpost, where customers grill their own steaks while swigging cold drinks in the swanky retro lounge. This freezer martini outsells all The Butterscotch Den's other cocktails combined, according to creative director and partner Trevor Easter, drawing in even those averse to gin or vermouth. It's a super-convenient home cocktail, as long as you have the freezer space. Make a batch ahead of time, stow it away and set it out for a couple of minutes to defrost as the mood strikes.

SERVES 9

Ingredients

1 1/3 cups Fords Gin

2/3 cup Dolin Dry Vermouth de Chambéry

2/3 cup Dolin Blanc Vermouth de Chambéry

1 1/2 cups filtered water

Directions

Combine ingredients in a bottle, give it a quick shake and store in the freezer. It will freeze solid, so let it sit out briefly to defrost before enjoying.

The Butterscotch Den
3406 Broadway, Sacramento
(916) 955-2556
thebutterscotchden.com

COURTESY OF THE BUTTERSCOTCH DEN

Bodega Kitchen & Cocktails

Hadyn's Choco-tiki-tini

A quick favorite in Greenhaven since opening in 2022, Bodega serves up Cali-Caribbean food and drinks with a slight emphasis on Puerto Rico, where co-founder Rafael Jimenez Rivera's grandfather once ran a restaurant (his dad also owned a Puerto Rican restaurant in New York City). Jimenez Rivera's business partners Chris Sinclair and Emily Neuhauser run the exploratory bar program as well as the carefully curated Good Bottle Shop in downtown Sacramento, which is preparing to move to midtown. This tropical riff on a chocolate martini, though, can be credited to bartender Hadyn George Tavarez. Unique and filled with panache, it's equal parts sweet, spice and looking nice.

SERVES 1

Ingredients

2 ounces KoHana Kokoleka rum

1 ounce oat milk

3/4 ounce cinnamon syrup

2 dashes cacao bitters

1 teaspoon hot cocoa mix

2 chocolate disks to garnish

Gold luster dust to garnish

Directions

1. Shake the rum, oat milk, cinnamon syrup, bitters and hot cocoa mix in a shaker with ice. Fine strain into a chilled coupe glass.

2. Dust the chocolate disks with the gold luster. Garnish and serve.

> ### Bartender's notes
>
> Good Bottle Shop carries cacao- and honey-infused KoHana Kokoleka rum, though Sinclair says home bartenders can substitute Copalli Cacao or Kōloa Kaua'i Cacao if those are easier to find. Gold luster dust is edible and can be ordered online.

144

XAVIER MASCAREÑAS / THE BEE

Bodega Kitchen & Cocktails
6401 Riverside Blvd., Sacramento
(916) 898-2231
bodegasac.com

KEVIN NERI / THE BEE

Bottle & Barlow

Kiss & Tell

Hair guru Anthony Giannotti and bartender Jayson Wilde combined their crafts with Bottle & Barlow. Half barber shop, half cocktail lounge, it's become a hotspot in Sacramento's bustling R Street Corridor thanks to a rotating menu of inventive, cleverly named cocktails and mocktails. The Kiss & Tell is the drink that started it all, the first cocktail Wilde had Giannotti taste before they opened Bottle & Barlow in 2015. Crushable and delicious, it's become the best-known menu item in years since.

SERVES 1

Ingredients

1 1/2 ounces vodka

1/2 ounce Aperol

1/2 ounce pineapple syrup

3 1/2 ounces fresh lemon juice

2 ounces club soda

Cucumber slice to garnish

Directions

1. Combine the vodka, Aperol, pineapple syrup and lemon juice in a shaker. Shake and pour over ice in a Collins glass.

2. Top with club soda and garnish with the cucumber slice.

147

Bottle & Barlow

1120 R St., Sacramento

(916) 379-7719

bottleandbarlow.com

La Sandia

It's hard to miss La Sandia at Midtown's Cantina Alley. Inspired by the green, white and red of Mexico's flag, the shareable margarita comes in a hollowed-out watermelon, straws shooting out of its Tajín rim towards thirsty mouths. It's an appropriately summery cocktail for this open-air restaurant and bar, which debuted between J and K streets on 23rd Street in 2017. General manager Oscar Escobar has been the chief mixologist all the while, crafting the cocktails that have made Cantina Alley a Latino hotspot enjoyed by midtown partiers of all backgrounds.

SERVES 2

Ingredients

5-pound watermelon

4 1/2 ounces tequila

2 ounces fresh lime juice

2 ounces agave nectar

1/2 cup water

Tajín to garnish

Directions

1. Using a sharp knife, cut off the top of the watermelon, going about a 1/2-inch deep into the red part of the fruit. Cut the inside of the fruit in a grid-like pattern, creating 1/2-inch squares. Cut the outside pieces away from the rind, leaving a small layer of watermelon attached to the white of the rind. Using a spoon, scoop out the cut pieces of watermelon and place into a sealable container.

2. Place 2 cups of the watermelon in a blender along with the water and blend until combined. Pour into a glass pitcher or another container using a fine mesh strainer.

3. Combine the watermelon solution, tequila, lime juice and agave nectar in a cocktail shaker with ice and shake until thoroughly mixed, about 40 seconds. Pour directly into the carved watermelon and add more ice to your liking.

4. Sprinkle the rim of the watermelon with Tajín (or "Mexican glitter," as Escobar calls it). Garnish with a remaining slice of watermelon, add straws and enjoy.

148

Midtown's Cantina Alley
2320 Jazz Alley, Sacramento
(833) 232-0639
cantinaalley.com

JOSÉ LUIS VILLEGAS / THE BEE

The Snug

Mechanical bull

Pub charm meets downtown cocktail bar at The Snug, Irish Hospitality Group's dark wood joint in the R Street Corridor. Named for the side rooms in many British and Irish pubs, The Snug debuted in 2019 with family photos, notebooks for menus and an impressive selection of booze. It's not the right vibe for an actual mechanical bull, but this cocktail has managed to stay on the menu since opening nonetheless. A bold, punchy take on a whiskey sour, it's the perfect drink to get you revved up and ready to take on the night, Irish Hospitality creative director and partner Trevor Easter says.

SERVES 1

Ingredients

1 ounce bourbon

1/2 ounce Fernet-Branca

3/4 ounce fresh lemon juice

3/4 ounce ginger syrup

Ginger candy to garnish

Directions

1. To make ginger syrup, juice fresh ginger or purchase the juice from a local shop. Combine the juice with white sugar at a 1 part ginger juice to 1 1/2 parts sugar ratio, and blend until sugar has dissolved.

2. Combine ingredients in a shaker with ice and shake like hell. Strain over new ice in a rocks glass and garnish with ginger candy.

The Snug
1800 15th St., Suite F, Sacramento
snugca.com

COURTESY OF THE SNUG

The Flamingo House and Darling Aviary

Paloma

Bobby Falcon, Matt Byrd — these bar owners had little choice but to give their establishments a bird theme, along with partner Christian Tolen. The Flamingo House came first, a converted pink Victorian with a tropical bent that's become one of midtown Sacramento's buzziest spots for a night out since opening in 2017. This Jarritos-topped paloma was the first cocktail The Flamingo House's owners and staff came up with, and it's been the top-selling concoction ever since. It's also carried over to Darling Aviary, the partners' multi-story rooftop bar overlooking Downtown Commons and Golden 1 Center that opened in 2020.

SERVES 1

Ingredients

1 1/2 ounces Dulce Vida Grapefruit Tequila

1/2 ounce lime juice

1/2 ounce lemon juice

1/2 ounce agave syrup

2 ounces Jarritos Mandarin soda

1 dehydrated grapefruit peel moon to garnish

1 edible flower to garnish

152

Directions

1. Combine tequila, lime and lemon juices and agave syrup in a shaker and shake vigorously. Double strain into a chilled Collins glass filled to the brim with ice.

2. Top off with Jarritos Mandarin and garnish with grapefruit moon and edible flower.

Bartender's notes

Dehydrated grapefruit wheels can be bought through online retailers such as Amazon, or made at home. To do the latter, slice the peels 1/4-inch thick and leave them in a 135-degree oven for about 8 hours. You can also substitute with fresh grapefruit peels cut into half-moon wheels. Edible flowers can be found at local farmers markets or the Sacramento Natural Foods Co-op.

The Flamingo House
2315 K St., Sacramento
(916) 409-7500
flamingohousesac.com

Darling Aviary
712 K St., Sacramento
(916) 758-5715
darlingaviary.com

SARA NEVIS / THE BEE

SARA NEVIS / THE BEE

COURTESY OF THE SHADY LADY SALOON

The Shady Lady Saloon

White Linen

Sacramento's signature cocktail is a refreshing, light balm born for sweaty summer days. Concocted by then-Shady Lady/Ella Dining Room & Bar bartender Rene Dominguez during the 2008 Sacramento Cocktail Week, the White Linen has taken on a reputation of its own, with imitators trying their own versions around the city. It's still the drink to get at Jason Boggs, Alex Origoni and Garrett Van Vleck's semi-swanky R Street Corridor restaurant and bar, which pays tribute to the Roaring 20s. Local grocery chain Raley's even stocks a just-add-booze White Linen mixer, but it's more fun and tastier to drink at The Shady Lady — or make your own from scratch.

SERVES 1

Ingredients

1 1/2 ounces gin

1 ounce lemon juice

1/2 ounce simple syrup

1/2 ounce elderflower liqueur

Soda water to taste

3–4 cucumber slices to garnish

Directions

1. Combine all liquids except the soda water in a shaker. Add ice and shake.

2. Pour over new ice in a Collins glass, then top off with soda water and garnish with cucumber slices.

155

The Shady Lady Saloon
1409 R St., Sacramento
(916) 231-9121
shadyladybar.com

KEVIN NERI / THE BEE

Index

NOTE: Page numbers in *italics* indicate a photograph.

Acknowledgments

The idea for this cookbook came to me on the long, dull drive from Los Angeles back to Sacramento in September 2021. Turning it into a reality required the generosity, inspiration and support of many others.

This book hinged on Sacramento-area chefs' willingness to share their proprietary recipes. Time and again, I was surprised and touched by their eagerness to do so. Many of those chefs, restaurateurs and bar managers are mentioned along with their recipes; those that are not include Casey Willard (Séka Hills), Ben Horpedahl (Selland's Market-Cafe), Karen Knudson (Jimboy's Tacos) and Trevor Easter (The Snug). The restaurant industry has always been difficult, and the last few years have been particularly challenging for many Sacramento institutions. I encourage readers to make the dishes described in this cookbook, then visit their corresponding restaurants to try more.

I'm not sure this book would have gotten off the ground without my inclusion in the Poynter-Koch Media & Journalism Fellowship, which asked fellows to conceive of "innovation projects" to better our newsrooms or communities. This cookbook was my project, though it was far from a solo effort. Kristen Hare helped guide me through the transition from newspaper writing to book publishing. Benét J. Wilson taught me how to market myself and this book without feeling gross about it. The ever-cheerful Gil Asakawa taught me lessons of cultural competency every time we spoke.

Few journalists are fortunate enough to write a book on company time. The Sacramento Bee supported this venture in words and actions, starting from the top of the masthead with Colleen McCain Nelson, Scott Lebar and Alvie Lindsay. Emilie Stigliani, my newsroom editor for most of the project, led with open ears, a critical eye and a compassionate soul. Most of the beautiful photographs between these pages came from Xavier Mascareñas, Hector Amezcua, Renée C. Byer, Paul Kitagaki Jr., Kevin Neri and Lezlie Sterling, as coordinated by visuals editor Nathaniel Levine. Sonora Slater, Grace Scullion and Ellie Lin provided invaluable fact-checking support, verifying key details to make this book accurate and precise.

When it came time to find a publishing house, I reached out directly to Pediment Publishing, whose sterling reputation for working with reporters and newsrooms preceded them. Chris Fenison was a breeze to work with, offering the kind of direct communication and responsiveness one wouldn't find from the head of a larger publisher. Many recipes in this book came from family owned restaurants, and I'm glad that it was published by a family owned business as well.

Past editors including Kayla Missman, Adam Ashton, Donald Winslow, Chris Saur, Jim Patrick, Anthony Sorci and Ryan Lillis have shaped not just my stories, but my career and my life. My educators within Cal Poly, San Luis Obispo's journalism department deserve special mention as well, particularly Pat Howe, Teresa Allen, Mary Glick, Brady Teufel and Bill Loving. My sister Naomi Egel was my first teacher, overseeing a classroom of me and her teddy bears long before she became a college professor, and continues to inspire me with her passion and work ethic. She's also become an adventurous diner in her own right, evolving from eating cheese pizza sans sauce to ordering the one food I won't touch (escargot).

Food has the power to connect people with cultures, whether that be finding one's own roots or learning about a far-off way of life. No one taught me that more than my grandmother Judy Bacskai, who fled Communist Hungary with my grandfather after surviving the Holocaust. I came around long after they had built new, full lives together in Northern California, and grew up treated to my grandmother's uborkasaláta (pickled cucumber salad) and rakott káposzta (sausage and sauerkraut casserole) along with her meatloaf and matzo ball soup. She's been as essential to my culinary education as any professional chef, teaching me the power of food as nourishment, family connection and an expression of love.

To Abbey Warner: Meals taste better with you as my dining companion. I'm deeply grateful for your emotional support, problem-solving skills and willingness to split dishes when we go out to eat. Sweet Pea and Poppy constantly remind me that there is no purer love than that of a dog, as does the memory of Truffles.

Finally, I couldn't wish for better parents than my biggest fans, Rob and Dotti Egel. You're my guiding lights. I'll leave readers with the same concise advice my mom gives me every time I head out for the night: Be good, be nice, be safe, have fun.

CHEERS,
BENJY EGEL

Pediment Publishing, a division of The Pediment Group, Inc., Vancouver, Washington 98682
www.pediment.com
© 2023 by The Sacramento Bee
All Rights Reserved. Published 2023.
Printed in Canada.

Library of Congress Control Number: 2023914388
ISBN: 978-1-63846-061-9